MILLENNIUM:
BEGINNING OR END?

Mark and Gail
all our Love,
Mom and Dad

2001

MILLENNIUM: BEGINNING OR END?

by Jack Van Impe

WORD PUBLISHING

NASHVILLE

A Thomas Nelson Company

Published by Word Publishing, a unit of Thomas Nelson, Inc., P. O.
Box 14100, Nashville, Tennessee 37214. No portion of this book may
be reproduced, stored in a retrieval system, or transmitted in any form
or by any means—electronic, mechanical, photocopy, recording, or
other—except for brief quotations in printed reviews, without the prior
permission of the publisher.

Scripture quotations used in this book are from The King James
Version of the Bible.

Library of Congress Cataloging-in-Publication Data

Van Impe, Jack.
    Millennium: beginning or end? / by Jack Van Impe.
        p. cm.
    ISBN 0-8499-4072-9
    1. Millennialism. I. Title.
    BT891.V35 1999
    236'.9—dc21   99-38050
                                                                    CIP

Printed in the United States of America

99 00 01 02 03 04 QPV 6 5 4 3 2 1

CONTENTS

Foreword vii

Prelude to the Future xiii

CHAPTER 1
Laying the Foundation 1

CHAPTER 2
The Controversy Continues 23

CHAPTER 3
The Glorious Second Coming of Jesus Christ 41

CHAPTER 4
The Great Campaign 57

CHAPTER 5
The Millennial Judgment 71

CONTENTS

CHAPTER 6

A Government of Righteousness   91

CHAPTER 7

The Spiritual Environment of the Millennium   109

CHAPTER 8

Life in the Millennium: *A View from Above*   129

CHAPTER 9

The Heavenly Jerusalem   151

CHAPTER 10

The Final Days   169

Appendix   187
Notes   199

FOREWORD

It was only 5:15 in the afternoon, and the parking lot was already full. The evening service wasn't to begin until 6:00 P.M. Soon cars were parking on the grass, in the woods, down by the pole barn, and even on the vacant property next door. What was happening?

Ushers were bustling about, frantically setting up more chairs to squeeze in another thousand people. Big-screen projectors were set up in overflow areas as thousands smashed their way into our Lansing, Michigan, church. Another hundred people stood on the balcony until the ushers created yet another makeshift, overflow area where they could be seated. What was going on?

It seemed like Acts 13:44 was becoming a reality: "And the next sabbath day came almost the whole city together to hear the word of God."

By 5:45 P.M. thousands had already crowded into the building. We wondered if the whole city was coming.

Everyone bubbled with excitement and anticipation. Nobody seemed to complain, even though traffic was backing up, people sat shoulder to shoulder, and the temperature rose as the old air conditioners worked their best to keep the auditorium bearable.

What was happening? It's simple. Dr. Jack Van Impe was our speaker that night. The people were especially excited because they knew that Jack doesn't make public appearances *unless* the Spirit of God speaks directly to his heart. So thousands came out that night to hear this trusted man of God who has earned the reputation of being the most listened-to, authoritative voice in Bible prophecy today. Best of all, at Dr. Van Impe's gospel invitation, hundreds met Jesus Christ as their Savior and Lord on that unforgettable night in Lansing, Michigan, at Mount Hope Church.

Why do so many pastors and laypeople alike look to Jack Van Impe for prophetic insight into God's Word? It's simply because he can be trusted to present God's Word accurately, authoritatively, and in a simple, easy-to-understand manner. In a nutshell, he makes learning a joy.

Dr. Jack Van Impe has been preaching the gospel of Jesus Christ for more than fifty years. I have been acquainted with Dr. Jack and Rexella Van Impe's ministry for nearly half of those fifty years. During the past years, Mary Jo and I have become wonderful friends with these dear people. And once you have Jack and

Rexella for friends, you have friends for life. We love, admire, and highly esteem these dear servants of Christ who touch many millions of lives every week.

I am thrilled to write the foreword for Jack's new book, *Millennium: Beginning or End?* Through the centuries, there has been unbelievable controversy concerning the Millennium. Now, at last, we can enjoy a scholarly look at what the Bible *really* teaches about this thousand-year reign of Christ. Millions of sincere people, even dedicated Christians, misunderstand the doctrine of the Millennium.

I have heard some interesting concepts regarding the Millennium. I have heard that we Christians must establish the Millennial Kingdom before Christ can return. I have heard that there will be no Millennium at all. I even heard a preacher proclaiming to his audience that the Millennium doctrine is nonsense, that Jesus will only return "in spirit" after Christians rise up and take over the world. I get a gut-wrenching pain in the pit of my stomach when I hear these unscriptural teachings being propagated. Perhaps these people are sincere; I don't know. But I *do* know that you can be sincere and still be wrong—dead wrong!

On the other hand, when I listen to Jack's prophetic presentations, I have a sense of security, knowing the depth of his painstaking, prayerful research. Here's a man who has devoted his life to "rightly dividing the word of truth" (2 Timothy 2:15).

I know Jack's life. I know his integrity. I know his example. I know his love for the Savior (and I might add, his love for his precious wife, Rexella). Like the Ephesians, addressed by Jesus in Revelation chapter two, Jack has no tolerance for so-called apostles or prophets who twist and corrupt God's Word (2 Corinthians 4:2). And that makes me feel safe. Without reservation, I enthusiastically encourage members of our church to watch *Jack Van Impe Presents,* to study his books, and to watch his videos (which, by the way, have been viewed by more than 60 million people). As a pastor, I'm never afraid that Jack will lead my flock down a crooked road. I view him as a pastor's helper.

A dear pastor once told me, "I've never taught on Bible prophecy because I don't understand it." Yet one-third of the Bible is prophetic. And God meant for us to study and understand it. Jesus said, "It is given unto you to know the mysteries of the kingdom" (Matthew 13:11).

We *can* know and understand Bible prophecy as it relates to God's kingdom and the future. But it takes digging—plenty of digging. It's rather like mining for precious metals or diamonds. Jack Van Impe is a miner. His relentless study of the Bible, his never-ending quest for revelation, and his unswerving commitment to the trustworthiness of God's written Word have led him to some of the greatest prophetic mining "finds" in the world today. And the beautiful thing is this: Jack is willing to unselfishly share his treasures *with us* through television, videotapes, and books like this. What a blessing for a pastor like me to have a researcher like Dr. Jack Van Impe.

Others feel the same.

The famous radio preacher the late Dr. C. M. Ward, who had heard his share of "fad prophecy doctrines," spoke often of his personal admiration for Dr. Jack Van Impe. He appreciated Jack's careful, well-researched, well-defined, always dependable presentations of prophetic truth. Dr. Ward valued Dr. Van Impe's masterful and scholarly approach to Bible prophecy.

Peter Lalonde, a well-known Canadian Christian broadcaster and film producer, stated, "Jack Van Impe is not merely *a* prophetic voice in the Church world; he is now *the* prophetic voice." He was referring to Jack being the authoritative and dependable voice in prophecy today for the Church of Jesus Christ. I agree. And it's largely because of his unyielding commitment to present the prophetic truth, based *only* upon the sure foundation of God's eternal Word—the Bible (Matthew 24:35).

Yes, people everywhere are crying out to hear an authoritative voice on biblical prophecy. Dr. Jack Van Impe *is* that voice. That's why people will stand in line, park in vacant lots, and press in to hear what he has to say, even if it means they'll have to stand for two or more hours. But *you* won't have to stand today to hear Dr. Van Impe's voice. You can sit back, relax, and hear his voice, along with the voice of the Holy Spirit, as you read this enlightening and compelling revelation concerning the coming kingdom.

I am pleased to present to you Dr. Jack Van Impe's thirty-third full-length book.

Get ready to receive a fresh biblical discovery that will stir your faith. As you read this eye-opening book, *Millennium: Beginning or End?* you'll find the controversies that have clouded the doctrine of the Millennium will be cleared up, the waters will be "unmuddied," and a fresh light will penetrate your heart.

DAVE WILLIAMS
PASTOR, MOUNT HOPE CHURCH
Lansing, Michigan, 1999

PRELUDE TO THE FUTURE

Some people who patiently endure great trials are often ready to give up when faced with comparatively small ones. And when they do, it's both tragic and ironic. Charles Haddon Spurgeon, thinking along that line, related an incident about the swashbuckling English mariner Sir Francis Drake. The great preacher reflected, "Being in a dangerous storm in the Thames River, Drake was heard to say, 'Must I, who have escaped the rage of the ocean, be drowned in a ditch!'" Spurgeon then went on to make this application, "Will you, experienced saints, who have passed through a world of tribulation, lie down and die of despair, or give up your profession because you are at the present moment passing through some light affliction? Let your past preservation inspire you with courage and constrain you to brave all the storms for Jesus' sake."

What fitting words for the times in which you and I

live. Spurgeon had it right: *light afflictions* are what we have been compelled to endure. However, whatever afflictions and tribulations we may have experienced up to this point in our lives pale in comparison to the great trials and God-mandated Tribulation yet to come. The disconcerting news for those refusing to accept Jesus as Lord is that things will, indeed, get worse. The good news is that faithful followers of the Lord Jesus Christ will be caught away in the *twinkling of an eye,* forever removed from the monstrous terror still to come. And then what? Well, that is the subject of this book, *Millennium: Beginning or End?*—a thousand-year period that is much misunderstood, ignored, and even derided. Comedian Woody Allen once quipped that the Millennium would be a period in history when the lion might lie down with the lamb *but that the lamb wouldn't get much sleep.* Allen is wrong. Why? First, it's a wolf that lies down with the lamb, and secondly, the lamb *will* sleep because Christ is in control. The Millennium will be a thousand years of universal peace, utopian in the extreme. It will be a period when "they shall beat their swords into plowshares, and their spears into pruninghooks" (Isaiah 2:4). Why? Because the Prince of Peace is here (Isaiah 9:6). It will be a time of health.

Then the eyes of the blind shall be opened, and the ears of the deaf shall be unstopped. Then shall the lame man leap as an hart, and the tongue of the dumb sing: . . . And an highway shall be there, and a way, and it shall be called The way of holiness; the unclean shall not pass over it; but it shall be for those [righteous] . . . No lion shall be there, nor any ravenous beast shall go up thereon. (Isaiah 35:5-6, 8-9)

The earth's motto during the Millennium reign will be "HOLINESS UNTO THE LORD" (Zechariah 14:20). When Christ comes as King of kings and Lord of lords, He will also bear the supreme title of "The Holy One," or "His Holiness." Universal righteousness will flood the four corners of the world during this glorious hour. Everything will be calm, beautiful, and tranquil.

Meanwhile, for the most part, we sit naively on an economic powder keg. Explosive population growth in the countries that can least afford it will put one of the final nails in the coffin of nations already on the slippery slope of economic disaster. In many countries, land once fertile has succumbed to hot, blowing desert sand, depriving once highly productive countries of exportable commodities and making them recipients of the charity of donor nations.

The recent financial troubles throughout the nations of Asia begin to reveal the magnitude of the problem and its international effect. And the global travail is only beginning. The lead story in a recent issue of *Business Week* reports the health of the global economy is at stake. The article detailed the planning of the most complex bailout in history, combining the efforts of the International Monetary Fund, the World Bank, the U.S.

Treasury Department, private investment bankers, and large multinational banks—in a bailout of Asia, perhaps to the tune of more than $100 billion. However, analysts believe that Asia's bailout will not succeed unless the region's leaders change their habit of borrowing *far more money than could be prudently invested.* My friend, we teeter on the edge of one of the greatest moments in history.

Meanwhile, new global bureaucracies—from the World Trade Organization to the International Monetary Fund—are established to handle the growth of the world's new financial markets. Martin Waller, bureau chief of the *Guardian* in England, says that recent attempts by the G-7 nations (soon to be the G-8, with the addition of Russia) to tame the global markets may have the effect of "anointing a market pontiff whose reach transcends old sovereignties." Translation: The New Economic Order is coming. The apparatus is nearly in place for central planning on a global scale. However, as with most radical plans, *it will surely be preceded by a crisis of enormous proportions*—in all probability, a worldwide recession. Watch for it. Read the business section of your morning paper with the discernment that comes with "new eyes," because the signs of global economic chaos are on the horizon (Daniel 7:23; Revelation 18:10, 17, 19).

The truth of the future, however, has not been left unexplored by the wisdom of the past. In James 5:1-8, read one example of how the Bible has always been ahead of its time:

> Go to now, ye rich men, weep and howl for your miseries that shall come upon you. Your riches are corrupted, and your garments are motheaten. Your gold and silver is cankered; and the rust of them shall be a witness against you, and shall eat your flesh as it were fire. Ye have heaped treasure together for the last days. Behold, the hire of the labourers who have reaped down your fields, which is of you kept back by fraud, crieth: and the cries of them which have reaped are entered into the ears of the Lord of sabaoth. Ye have lived in pleasure on the earth, and been wanton; ye have nourished your hearts, as in a day of slaughter. Ye have condemned and killed the just; and he doth not resist you. Be patient therefore, brethren, unto the coming of the Lord. Behold, the husbandman waiteth for the precious fruit of the earth, and hath long patience for it, until he receive the early and latter rain. Be ye also patient; stablish your hearts; for the coming of the Lord draweth nigh.

My friend, the day of reckoning will soon be upon us, and then, after the terrible, sure-to-come seven years of Tribulation, the Millennium will begin, a time when our world will finally know the peace it has so long sought. However, before the first day of the thousand years appears, other earth-shattering, momentous events must rear their heads. We will deal with some of these happenings in the early chapters of this book, after which we will then take an intimate look at what life on earth will be like during the Millennium. I have been preparing to write this book for many years, and now it is with prayerful pen and grateful heart that I give this message of hope to you. May God bless and keep you strong as you read the pages that follow . . . and may my words help prepare you for the tumultuous days that lie ahead, events that must occur before our Lord returns in majesty, power, and strength to rule and reign with His chosen Bride for one thousand years.

"Watch ye therefore: for ye know not when the master of the house cometh, at even, or at midnight, or at the cockcrowing, or in the morning: Lest coming suddenly he find you sleeping. And what I say unto you I say unto all, Watch."
(Mark 13:35-37)

CHAPTER 1

LAYING THE FOUNDATION

It is not necessary for me to remind you that our world is unstable politically, physically, socially, morally, and spiritually. Our world teeters on the precipice of disaster with world leaders, along with rank-and-file citizens everywhere, doing whatever possible to bring our individual and corporate lives to the edge of unrestrained chaos. You already know this: you watch the news and you read the newspapers. What many fail to see, however, is just how close we really are to that great day when Jesus will return for His thousand-year earthly reign, a period of history when there shall be peace as the world has not known since the days of the Garden of Eden, before the Fall. The actual appearance of Christ will usher in unprecedented, momentous events as His rule extends over the entire earth. He will be King of kings and Lord of lords as He sits on the throne of David as the Son of David, ruling over Israel.

It is also important to recognize that the earthquake of impending geopolitical events comes as no surprise to the Lord Jesus Christ. For those who may have regarded the Bible as bogus, old-fashioned, and out of sync with the real world, I would submit one example of how we can be assured quite the exact opposite is true. Jesus' inner circle of disciples asked the Savior in Mark 13:4-7, "'Tell us, when shall these things be? and what shall be the sign when all these things shall be fulfilled?' And Jesus answering them began to say, 'Take heed lest any man deceive you: For many shall come in my name, saying, I am Christ; and shall deceive many. And when ye shall hear of wars and rumours of wars, be ye not troubled: for such things must needs be; but the end [of the age] shall not be yet.'"

British editor of the highly reliable *Intelligence Digest,* Joseph De Courcey, said in his recent newsletter that he believes "the general world situation is entering a period of instability such has not been seen since the end of World War II." He goes on to explain the five main reasons why he thinks this is the case. I have no doubt this writer and editor has hit the nail on the head.

> The general world situation is entering a period of instability such has not been seen since the end of World War II.
>
> —JOSEPH DE COURCEY

1. The collapse of the Soviet Union, like the collapse of any empire, has left the border regions in turmoil. This has led directly to the first war in Europe in over fifty years and could yet lead to further upsets.

2. The rise of China. Like the collapse of a great power, so the rapid rise of another fuels instability. In the case of China's rise, India has already reacted by joining the nuclear club, thus forcing Pakistan, in turn, down the same path. Next Japan's neighbors will respond to its rearming. And so it will go on.

3. The general instability consequent upon the collapse of the Soviet Union is now just being felt around its borders. In Africa, war is threatening to spread across the continent, with troops from Angola, Burundi, Chad (financed by Libya), Namibia, Rwanda, Uganda, and Zimbabwe all reported to be active in Congo.

4. The economic crisis which has spread from Asia via Russia to virtually the whole developing world now threatens the major economies of the industrialized West; and, in echoes of the 1930's, calls for protectionism are beginning to be heard. The crisis will be exacerbated by the ill-judged folding of 11 European currencies into one as from January 1999 (and also by falling confidence in the run-up to the year 2000 computer-bug deadline).

5. The Middle East. Of all the crises currently brewing, the Middle East is our greatest concern, partly because of its potential to escalate out of control—even to the extent of first use of nuclear weapons since 1945, and partly because of the number of major flash-points coming up in the next 12 months, including the proposed delivery of S-300 missiles to Cyprus (which could involve Turkey in a war with Greece and Russia, thus freeing Syria to attack Israel); Turkish elections which could return the Islamists to power with similar consequences; Yassar Arafat's threat to declare Palestinian statehood . . . (which could prompt an Israeli move to retake the West Bank and Gaza Strip with obvious consequences); and the likely deployment this time next year of Israel's anti-missile Arrow system which will go some way toward nullifying the immense Arab investment in missiles and which, therefore, provides an important incentive for an early pre-emptive strike.[1]

CONTINUED GLOBAL CONFUSION

Not a pretty picture, is it? Add to this general global condition the fact that in the year 2000, presidential elections are scheduled in the United States and in Russia. The pope in Rome is frail and aging. The heads of the Israeli government and the Palestinian Authority have humongous obstacles to solve. No Asian leader has yet to come forward with answers to the region's exploding financial crisis. There is a widely recognized, growing awareness of a leadership vacuum in the world today. People clamor for a powerful political figure to step up to the challenges of today's crises and to fill the void left by present ineffectual, weak heads of state.

Meanwhile, the infamous Antichrist (2 Thessalonians 2:3-10) may soon appear on the international scene. Logic dictates that this man is alive today, waiting to make his move. After his reign of terror plays out, however, the Bible tells us the next step in God's prophetic plan is the fulfillment of Jesus' promise to His disciples to come again, as recorded in Matthew 24. But before that glorious appearing, all hell will break loose on planet earth—a furious time of pain, mayhem, and agony for millions. But as terrible as it will be for those left behind, *there will still be hope*. That's because in the midst of the horrible global carnage and destruction of the world as we know it today, the greatest revival in history will occur (Joel 2:28-29; Acts 2:17-18; Revelation 7:9-14). And all who desire salvation during this time may experience it because "whosoever shall call on the name of the LORD shall be saved" (Joel 2:32; Acts 2:21).

> People clamor for a powerful political figure to step up to the challenges of today's crises and fill the void left by present ineffectual, weak heads of state.

WE KNOW THE END OF THE STORY

The good news is that there is always hope in Jesus, then and now. That's why I can say with confidence that if one is a child of God, there is no need to be sad, confused, or despondent as you "sit out" the next few years as history unfolds. How can I say this with such certainty? Because you and I *know the ending of the Book*. There will be no surprises. We know how the story concludes. For this reason, we who know Jesus as Savior and Lord cannot afford to carry an attitude of despair and foreboding into our churches, our workplaces, or our family lives. Instead, we have cause for great rejoicing. Why? Because Christ is coming to snatch us away in the twinkling of an eye (1 Corinthians 15:51-53) before the holocaust begins and then to return with us to earth seven years later.

> The Bible makes it clear that in the midst of this fiery judgment, there will be little expression of remorse: hearts will not be bent toward repentance. Few will seek forgiveness for murder, drug abuse, fornication, sexual promiscuity, or theft.

Yes, I know this is a book on the Millennium, but the *prelude* to that glorious one-thousand-year period of history when Jesus sits on the throne of David, ruling Israel in power and might, must be examined for us to understand the intricacies of this period of history when the wolf *will indeed* lie down next to the lamb (Isaiah 11:6). Known as the Great Tribulation, this terrible period of human history will be the most horrendous our world has ever seen—seven years of nonstop bombardment of evil and despair (Revelation 6–18). The Bible makes it clear that in the midst of this fiery judgment, there will be little expression of remorse: hearts will not be bent toward repentance. Few will seek forgiveness for murder, drug abuse, fornication, sexual promiscuity, or theft (Revelation 9:21). The Tribulation and the sequential judgments of God, all promised and predicted in the Scriptures, will fall like meteors on unrepentant humankind because of its blatant sins against the most holy God. It will be a time of widespread apostasy, something we are already seeing as never before, coupled with an unashamed, wholesale denial of biblical truth, laced with moral chaos, an acceleration of spiritism, widespread persecution, pestilence, and earthquakes. Yet, terrible as all this will be, God promises a threefold redemptive purpose for this period of human history:

1. to save and allow many Jews who will enter the Millennium to experience the fulfillment of the kingdom's promises to Israel made by God in the covenants;

2. to save a multitude of Gentiles who will then populate the Millennial Kingdom; and

3. to pour out judgment on unbelieving mankind and nations. The final forty-two months or three-and-one-half-year period is so terrifying that it is called the Great Tribulation (Revelation 7:14).

PEACEFUL AT THE START

There is good reason to believe that the first half of the Tribulation will be relatively calm and peaceful for this reason: because Jesus Christ, the Prince of Peace, is soon to return to set up His glorious kingdom on earth for one thousand years. However, Satan, the great counterfeiter and ultimate deceiver, known as the Antichrist, first presents himself to the world as the Messiah. To set the world up—so he may later accomplish his dastardly deeds—he initially comes across as the *final answer* to the world's most pressing problems. Not only will he make himself known to all the nations, but will also be universally accepted, loved, cherished, and regarded as the ultimate problem solver and the world will worship him (Revelation 13:8).

Here are some of the details of his arrival: This Antichrist comes into prominence and power by presenting a "peace program" to the nations. Within a short period, the contracts are signed and confirmed (Daniel 9:27). (For more information on these "agreements," I encourage you to read my book, *Daniel: Final End Time Mysteries Unsealed*, published by Word Publishing. In this volume, I go into considerable detail on how the great book of Daniel contains all one really needs to know about latter-day events.) We know, through the details given us by the Word of God, that in the midst of the seven-year period of mayhem, the Antichrist dishonors his treaties and makes the last forty-two months the bloodiest in world history. We may think our present wars, skirmishes, and capacity for human chaos are beyond what we can endure, but what we see today is an innocent prelude to the terror yet to come. The Tribulation is a time of incomparable judgment from God (Daniel 12:1; Joel 2:2; and Matthew 24:21) when a total of twenty-one judgments fall upon the earth. They constitute three series of seven each and are described as the seal, trumpet, and vial (or bowl) judgments. This is "the time of Jacob's trouble" (Jeremiah 30:7) and depicted in Revelation 6, 8, 9, 15, and 16. Revelation 8:7 and 9:18 clearly reveal a judgment of fire during the Tribulation. This coincides with Psalm 97:3; Isaiah 66:15; Ezekiel 20:47; Zephaniah 1:18; Malachi 4:1; and numerous other passages of Scripture. Both Old and New Testaments agree on a fiery, nuclear holocaust (Ezekiel 39:6 and Revelation 8:7; 9:18). However, as I state repeatedly throughout this book, the unequivocal counsel of Scripture promises that the Church will be evacuated before the Great Tribulation judgment begins. I will not spend a great deal of time going through the horrendous events of this period, except to remind you that we, as followers of the true Messiah, will be caught away, "no longer available" to endure the pain to be suffered by a lost, sinful, and dying world. The good news is that in the closing hours of the seven years of Tribulation, something happens that turns the world on its ear. It is called the Millennium, the thousand-year earthly reign of Jesus Christ—and that is what this book is all about.

> We may think our present wars, skirmishes, and capacity for human chaos are beyond what we can endure, but what we see today is an innocent prelude to the terror yet to come.

DEFINITION OF TERMS

Millennium comes from the Latin *mille* and *annus*: *mille* meaning "thousand," and *annus* "years." You can find this period of time described in Revelation 20:2-7. The Romans called it *chilia ete,* which also means one thousand years, so it has become regarded in some circles as the doctrine of chiliasm. However, whether known as millennialism or chiliasm, the reality of this thousand-year period is clearly revealed in God's Word.

Yet, through the centuries, many have twisted the truth by saying there will be no Millennium. Some of these individuals propose a theology called "a-Millennial," or without Millennium. There is no basis in biblical fact to espouse this view, and we will dismiss it for the erroneous thinking it is.

Later, other scholars developed what was called a post-Millennial theory. This is even more difficult to believe. The post-Millennium view suggests that the onus is on people like you and me to do all we can to make our world a better, safer place. It's all up to us. We are told we must burn the midnight oil to make our world right physically, spiritually, and morally and, by so doing, prepare it as one would prepare a birthday gift for Christ's return at the *end* of the thousand years. In my view, this is why so many are working feverishly today to try to *correct* the political situation both in America and throughout the world. I will not mention names, but one can find these groups under such labels as Christian Restorationists, Christian Restitutionists, and Dominionists.

While proponents of a post-Millennial view may be sincere in their attempts to work through this issue, and I do not fault them for their zeal, nowhere in the Bible does one find a single verse to fortify this position. My friend, the truth is that it is *not* going to get better. It is going to get worse and worse, and then even worse than that. In fact, Jesus said that just before He returns, iniquity will abound (Matthew 24:12). He said in Matthew 24:37, "As the days of No-e [Noah] were, so shall also the coming of the Son of man be." How was it during the days of Noah? Let's investigate. You will remember that the entire known world was filled with corruption and violence (Genesis 6:11-12). Would you not agree that we are already seeing such a trend? Also, 2 Timothy 3:13

says that just before Christ comes, "evil men and seducers shall wax worse and worse, deceiving, and being deceived." So, it is *not* getting better. It is getting worse. For this reason, I submit that the theories of both the a-Millennialists and post-Millennialists hold no water. The only position we dare take is the biblically sound pre-Millennial view. Simply restated, Jesus will return to earth *before the thousand years,* clearly described in Revelation 19, when He comes as King of kings and Lord of lords to set up His thousand-year kingdom.

> The truth is that it is not going to get better. It is going to get worse and worse, and then even worse than that. In fact, Jesus said that just before He returns, iniquity will abound.

PRE-MILLENNIALISM CONFIRMED BY THE CHURCH FATHERS

So really, better days are coming, but that era of global calm and equilibrium will occur solely under the physical earthly reign of our Lord Jesus. Now, was this the doctrine taught by the Church Fathers from the first through the fourth centuries? The great historian Edward Gibbon, author of the eighteenth-century literary masterpiece *The Decline and Fall of the Roman Empire,* reminds us that the ancient and popular doctrine of the Millennium was carefully taught by a succession of Church

Fathers . . . especially Justin Martyr and Irenaeus, who conversed *with the immediate disciples of the apostles.* This is crucial *live testimony,* the sort of "verification of the facts" any court of law would welcome as key evidence in a trial. In other words, the apostles had disciples, and those twelve apostles taught their disciples the same doctrine of a pre-Millennial return of Christ. From what we have researched—even in secular history—this point of view was the reigning sentiment among orthodox believers.

> **It is vital that we have sure footing when it comes to understanding the historical evidence of when Christ will come relative to the Millennial reign.**

During the first 300 years of Christian history, the Church Fathers taught that Christ would come back for a thousand-year reign. There were no other options. First of all, the great church historian Irenaeus, A.D. 140, said that he bore witness to the testimony of Papia, a close friend of the Apostle John who wrote the Gospel of John and the book of Revelation, informing the world that John had told him that all the apostles, mentioned in Matthew 10:1-4, with the exception of Judas, believed that Christ would come and set up His thousand-year kingdom. This is an important point, because it is vital that we have sure footing when it comes to understanding the historical evidence of when Christ will come relative to the Millennial reign. Bear with me as I list the names of the Church Fathers who were the foundation of the Church of Jesus Christ upon the earth and who vigorously taught pre-Millennialism—the view that Christ would indeed come *before* the thousand years. There was Barnabas, followed by Bartholomew, Hermes, Clement of Rome, Ignatius, Papia, Polycarp, Pontius, Justin Martyr, Melito, Hegesippus, Tatian, Irenaeus, Tertullian, Cyprian, Commodianus, Hypolytus, Victorinus, Methodius, and finally Lanctanius. As someone has said, *if one wants to know the truth, one must go back to his roots.*

Here again are comments by two of the early Church's most outspoken individuals. Justin Martyr once commented that *there would be a resurrection of the dead and a thousand-year reign in Jerusalem as the prophets Ezekiel and Isaiah declared.* To further bolster the pre-Millennial position, Irenaeus, Bishop of Lyons, said that "when this Antichrist shall have devastated all things in this world, he will reign for three years and six months [the final forty-two months of the seven-year period] and then sit in the temple at Jerusalem, and then the Lord will come from heaven, in the clouds, casting this man, the Antichrist, and those who follow him into the lake of fire (Revelation 19:20). But bringing in for the righteous the times of the kingdom, that is the [1000-year] rest of the hallowed seventh day, and thus restoring to Abraham the promised inheritance."[2]

Many in our day are less willing to stand firm for this

pre-Millennial view. However, such was not the case in the early life of the Christian Church. Both Justin and Irenaeus spoke confidently when they affirmed that "there are three classes of men: one, the heretics who deny the resurrection of the flesh, and the actual event of the Millennium. The second class of people—the exactly orthodox: those who asserted both the resurrection and the kingdom of Christ on the earth. And third, those believers who consented with the just and yet endeavored to allegorize and turn into a metaphor all those scriptures produced for a proper reign of Christ therefore agreeing with the heretics."[3] It is important to recognize that this third group consisted of believers, but because of their lack of belief in what the Bible had to say about the Millennium, they were also essentially identified as heretics, according to Justin and Irenaeus.

These men were the original Fathers of the Church, the scholars of Christianity, going back 1,700, 1,800, 1,900 and 2,000 years. Here then is where we discover our roots. Jesus said in Luke 24:44, "All things must be fulfilled, which were written in the law of Moses, and in the prophets, and in the psalms, concerning me." This statement refers not only to Christ's first coming, but also to the 1,817 texts that speak of His Second Coming. Men did not create these ideas. God wrote this Book. And through His servant He said, "All scripture is given by inspiration of God" (2 Timothy 3:16). The words "inspired by God," *theopneustus,* mean "God-breathed."

Our heavenly Father breathed every word upon the apostles as they wrote God's Holy Book. Second Peter 1:21 says that "holy men of God spake as they were moved by the Holy Ghost." You cannot get around it. God wrote these things, and in the chapters that follow we will see much additional proof that Jesus' return to earth is near, that it will indeed bring in a beautiful, serene millennial life to people on earth for ten centuries.

> There was not one dissenting voice among churchmen on the pre-Millennial position until the fifth century.

LITERAL, NOT ALLEGORICAL

I have given you a lengthy *apologetic* for the belief that pre-Millennialism is the *only* position worthy to hold. Not because I have chosen a theological "hobbyhorse" to ride, or even because I have a need to be right, but rather, because this view is consistent with the teachings of the early Church and the general counsel of Scripture. In A.D. 325, at the Council of Nicaea, 318 bishops gathered together from around the world and reaffirmed the doctrine of the thousand-year reign of Christ on earth. In fact, there was not one dissenting voice among churchmen on the pre-Millennial position until the fifth century. For 400 years, until the Council of Ephesus in A.D. 431, this is what the Church believed. Only then did the scholar Origen begin to treat the Scriptures as allegories. Everything suddenly became a symbol, its literal meaning hopelessly spiritualized into saying virtually nothing. Unfortunately, Origen communicated his bias to Ambrose who, following in Origen's footsteps, had a distinct hatred for the Jews. It is fascinating to see how this played out and how it influenced later history.

Ambrose was the teacher of Augustine, and history records that he is the one who brought the erroneous teaching of a-Millennialism into the Church. Augustine was literally brainwashed by Origen and Ambrose, two anti-Semites who said: "We must get rid of all this Jewish teaching."[4] And here's how they did it—using allegories and symbols. For instance, the interpretation of the word *Israel* became modified to mean "the Church." Furthermore, when the word *Jerusalem* appeared, its *new* meaning suddenly became "heaven."

This toying with the biblical texts is strange to the extreme, because when we look at Ezekiel 38 and 39, when Russia marches against Israel—and Israel is mentioned eighteen different times—we would need to picture the scene as Russia invading the churches globally. This simply does not fit with the meaning of the text. Nor would the words make sense in Romans 10:1-2 where Paul says, "Brethren, my heart's desire and prayer to God for Israel is, that they might be saved. For I bear them record that they have a zeal of God, but not according to knowledge." If we were to use their erroneous interpretation, it would read: *My heart's desire and prayer to God for the church is that the church might get saved.* Here's the rub: no one can become a member of the Church of Jesus Christ without salvation (Acts 2:41; 47). Simply stated, the allegorical method is wrong. Why do I seem to belabor this? Because the biblical concept of Christ returning *before* the Millennium is vital to a proper understanding of each sequence of events yet to occur. Christ must come after the Great Tribulation and at the beginning of the thousand years of global peace and harmony. It's in the Book!

> Christ must come after the Great Tribulation and at the beginning of the thousand years of global peace and harmony.

THE RABBIS SPEAK

Here is an additional word of confirmation from recorded history. First this question: Where did the early Church Fathers get their concept of a pre-Millennial position? From the Jewish rabbis who held to a literal interpretation of the Old Testament. We can go back 2,200 years, 200 years before the birth of Christ, and some years later, and demonstrate what the great fathers of Judaism taught. I am talking about such historical luminaries as Rabbi Akiba, Rabbi Katina, Rabbi Bechai, Rabbi Elias, Rabbi Eliezer, Rabbi Isaac, and Rabbi Jose.

Each taught that the Messiah would return and set up His kingdom in Jerusalem (Zechariah 8:3; 14:16). It says that they shall come up "from year to year" to Jerusalem. For what purpose? "To worship the King." Who is this King? The Lord of hosts.

The rabbis went even further. They also taught the six-day theory of creation as a model for Christ's return to earth, one that the majority of the Church Fathers also adopted, which meant that the Messiah would come sometime shortly after the year 2000. They took their position from Psalm 90:4. "For a thousand years in thy sight are but as yesterday," or a day is like a thousand years. They then reasoned if the world had been created in six days (Genesis 1:31), and God rested on the seventh day (Genesis 2:2), that this would then be an accurate picture of man's time on earth before Christ's return. The time from Adam's creation to Christ's birth covered a period of 4,000 years, which they reasoned to be four days. *For a day is as a thousand years.* From the time of Christ's birth until now another two days or 2,000 years has transpired. When factored into the 6,000-year period, we must conclude that time is almost up. The six days will soon be completed and the Messiah will return.

All these Church Fathers I have quoted not only taught a literal thousand-year reign of Christ on earth, but also instructed their people that it would begin sometime after the year 2000. Because of differences in the world's calendars, it could begin anywhere from 2001 to

2012, and some scholars have estimated as long as 2020. Now I personally do not promote date setting because Jesus said in Matthew 24:33, you will "know that it is near, even at the doors," but you will not know the day nor the hour (verse 36). My friend, we are on the cusp of seeing the next major phase of biblical prophecy unfold before our eyes. The King is coming.

> As we continue to explore this great future event, it is my prayer that your heart will be blessed and encouraged, even as you realize the immediacy of what is about to happen to our world.

Meanwhile, Satan remains alive, working his mischief in the hearts of men and women throughout the earth. However, he is not in control. His ultimate fate is sealed. He is a "lame-duck" devil. Powerful for only a short time longer, he will be *removed from office*. This is why you and I must now focus our hearts and our lives on the Lord's return. The "signs" have never been more obvious. The Tribulation is near. That is the bad news for those who choose not to honor God and become His child. The good news, however, is that believers will not endure the pain and pangs of the twenty-one plagues soon to afflict pain on the earth because Jesus may come at any moment to take His Church to Himself. Then, at the close of the Great Tribulation, He will return in power and majesty with

His people to rule the earth for a thousand years (Jude, verse 14; Revelation 19:14).

As we continue to explore this great future event, it is my prayer that your heart will be blessed and encouraged, even as you realize the immediacy of what is about to happen in our world—events that will reshape our planet beyond recognition. But do not fear, for Jesus said, "Peace I leave with you, my peace I give unto you: not as the world giveth, give I unto you. Let not your heart be troubled, neither let it be afraid" (John 14:27). This is the *blessed hope* for which we wait, watch, and pray daily.

Blessed is he that readeth, and they that hear the words of this prophecy, and keep those things which are written therein.
(Revelation 1:3)

CHAPTER 2

THE CONTROVERSY CONTINUES

⁂

There was once a young farmer who was among the best in the county. He had more than a green thumb: it was as if he had a green body. Everything he planted grew and grew well. His stalks of corn were the highest; his kernels of wheat the fullest and most golden; his barley and oats were the talk of the township. But not only was the young man a good farmer, he was also a new Christian—a fervent follower of Jesus, eager to do his Master's bidding. One day while toiling in the field, he noticed what seemed to be a sudden movement of the clouds. He had never before seen such a phenomenon, and it caught his attention. He stopped his tractor, shaded his eyes from the blazing noonday sun, and noticed the clouds were slowly spelling out three letters: *G-P-C*. He was puzzled momentarily at what he saw, and then finally let out a loud "Hallelujah!" He ran back into the house, took out his Bible, dropped to his knees, and thanked

God for the personal message *G-P-C*, interpreted by our young farmer as "Go Preach Christ." And preach Christ he did. He sold his farm, gathered his belongings, and arranged to attend a nearby Bible school. He was not the best student in his class, but he was surely one of the most enthusiastic. When the time came to graduate, he had already been offered a pastorate in a small rural church. His time had finally come, and no one was more excited than this farmer-turned-preacher. His first sermon, however, was a disaster. He hemmed and hawed, mispronounced words, spoke too long, and mumbled. Not only did he put the congregation to sleep, but several members even left midsermon, unimpressed with the young man's delivery. The second sermon was even more discouraging. It was the same with the third, the fourth, and the fifth. Nothing seemed to work. Even the young man began to question his call. One evening one of the deacons knocked on the young pastor's office door and asked for a word with him.

"Come in," said a timid voice from inside.

"Good afternoon, pastor. I just wanted to talk to you for a few minutes."

"Are you going to ask for my resignation?"

"No, but I *am* going to ask you an important question. You know how you told us about how God assembled some clouds a few years ago while you were farming?"

"Sure. The clouds spelled out the letters *G-P-C.*—'Go

Preach Christ.' It's what has kept me going during these difficult months. It was an essential part of my call to Christian service."

"Yes, I know. And we were always impressed with your story and how it motivated you. But I think I need to say something, pastor. Did you ever consider that what God *really* meant to tell you was, 'Go Plow Corn'?"

THE TWO KINGDOMS:
KNOWING THE DIFFERENCE

Three letters, *G-P-C,* two distinctly different interpretations. And this is the same conflict we often have with understanding the Millennium. The conflict in interpretation, however, usually rears its head when one's personal bias or prejudice takes precedence over the literal words of Holy Scripture. In chapter 1, we demonstrated how many throughout history have manipulated Scripture for their own benefit, emasculated its message, and attempted to persuade entire generations that the idea of a Millennium in which Christ reigns supreme is merely symbolic and meaningless. In this chapter, I want to shed light on how one needs to be vigilant in one's understanding of Scripture.

I begin with a few familiar passages from God's Word, beginning with John 3:3 where we read, "Except a man be born again, he cannot see the kingdom of

God." Verse 5 says, "Except a man be born of water and of the Spirit, he cannot enter into the kingdom of God." Second Corinthians 5:8 reminds us "to be absent from the body, and to be present with the Lord." This verse clearly speaks about our going to heaven to be with the Lord when we die. These texts refer to the kingdom of God. Conversely, millions, perhaps billions, of Christians throughout the centuries have prayed the prayer Jesus taught His disciples to pray in Matthew 6:10, "Thy kingdom come. Thy will be done in earth, as it is in heaven."

> The conflict in interpretation, however, usually rears its head when one's personal bias or prejudice takes precedence over the literal words of Holy Scripure.

Obviously this cannot be the kingdom of God *in* heaven, because the kingdom of God, as requested in the prayer, is coming *from* heaven to earth—and, I may add, is coming soon. *The two kingdoms are not the same.* Now let's look at this second kingdom. Revelation 11:15 says, "The kingdoms of this world are become the kingdoms of our Lord." There can be no confusion here. You see, when Christ comes back to earth to begin the Millennium, He assumes the title of King of kings because He controls all the kings and kingdoms of the world (Revelation 19:16). This is the Word of God—pure and undefiled. There can be no other interpretation.

Skeptics also argue that Millennialists confuse the program of salvation for the two kingdoms. How wrong!

> We teach that the Holy Spirit, the third member of the Trinity, is God, omnipresent—everywhere at all times—and that He cannot be evacuated.

The messages of entrance into the kingdom of God and the kingdom of heaven are identical. Here's proof. Acts 10:43, "To [Christ] give all the [Old Testament] prophets witness, that through his name whosoever believeth in him shall receive remission of sins." In Matthew 3:1-2 we read, "In those days came John the Baptist, preaching in the wilderness of Judaea, and saying, Repent ye: for the kingdom of heaven is at hand." John the Baptist did not exclude the cross as some suggest. Instead in John 1:29, he observes Jesus Christ and says, "Behold the Lamb of God, which taketh away the sin of the world." Now, how did Christ take away the sin of the world? Only by the shedding of His blood. There is no other way of salvation in any dispensation. In Hebrews 10:4 and 5, Christ states: "It is not possible that the blood of bulls and of goats should take away sins . . . but a body hast [my Father] prepared me."

Stay with me as we build our case. Jews in the Old Testament knew one could not get to heaven without the shedding of blood. That is why Leviticus 17:11 says that "it is the blood that maketh an atonement for the soul."

The message of the shed blood of God's lamb appears seven hundred times in both Testaments as the only way of salvation. (See Acts 20:28; Ephesians 1:7; 1 John 1:7; and Revelation 1:5.) Now concerning this message of Christ's sacrifice at Calvary, it is impossible for anyone to come to Christ without the Holy Spirit's call (Revelation 22:17). However, certain a-Millennial detractors mock the idea of a great revival occurring during the Tribulation hour because of the Holy Spirit's absence on earth during that period of time. So they accuse pre-Millennialists of teaching that the Holy Spirit will be removed from the scene during this seven-year period and then mockingly continue their attack by questioning how the greatest revival in history is able to take place without the Holy Spirit's presence.

Get ready for a shock—neither I nor most pre-Millennialists believe that the Holy Spirit will be evacuated for the Tribulation period. We teach that the Holy Spirit, the third member of the Trinity, is God, omnipresent—everywhere at all times—and that He cannot be evacuated. Psalm 139:7-11 teaches that the Holy Spirit is in heaven, on earth, in the depths of the sea, and even in Hades. He is everywhere at all times because He is God—the third member of the Trinity. Misunder-standing comes when one misinterprets 2 Thessalonians 2:7, which says, "For the mystery of iniquity doth already work: only he who now letteth [hinders] will let [hinder], until he be taken out of the way." This is not the Spirit's personal removal, which is impossible. Instead, it is the departure of His restraining influence during the Tribulation hour. Now what is this influence? Spirit-filled believers. You see, when you and I are born again, the Holy Spirit comes into our bodies. "Except a man be born of water and of the Spirit, he cannot enter into the kingdom of God" (John 3:5). That's why the Bible says that our bodies are God's building, the Holy Spirit's dwelling place. First Corinthians 3:16 asks: "Know ye not that ye are the temple of God, and that the Spirit of God dwelleth in you?" First Corinthians 6:19 also asks a question, "Know ye not that your body is the temple of the Holy Ghost which is in you . . . ?" And because He is in us and we are the light of the world and the salt of the earth (Matthew 5:13-14), we are taken to be with the Lord during the Tribulation hour. At this point, the restraining influence of the Holy Spirit is removed (believers) while the Holy Spirit remains because, as God, He can never be removed from earth, sea, heaven, or hell (Psalm 139:7-11). This is an important theological position to understand as we further establish the scenario for the coming of the Millennium and Christ's return to earth accompanied by His people.

TWO KINDS OF ELECT ON THIS EARTH

Many of us learned 2 Timothy 2:15 while we were young, a verse that compels us to "rightly [divide] the word of truth." Keeping that verse in mind, let us recognize that there are two distinctly different groups of *elect people* upon this earth. In Matthew 24:21-22 we read, "For then shall be great tribulation, such as was not since the beginning of the world to this time, no, nor ever shall be. And except those days should be shortened, there should no flesh be saved: but for the elect's sake those days shall be shortened." Does this mean that the Christian elect will be present during the Great Tribulation? No. God has two elect groups. Yahweh's wife, Israel (Jeremiah 3:14), and Christ's Bride, the Church (Revelation 19:7-8). The Church is Christ's elect according to Ephesians 1:4 and 1 Peter 1:2; however, there's another elect group. The words of Isaiah 42:1; 45:4; 65:9; and 65:22 remind us that Yahweh God says, Israel is "mine elect." And it is this elect group for whom God shortens the days (Matthew 24:22). Here's how we can know this to be true. This elect group, according to Matthew 24:16, is fleeing from Judea to the mountains. Remember that Judea is located in Israel. In verse 20, Jesus warns them not to flee on the Sabbath. We Christians do not worship on the seventh day, Sabbath, but rather on the first day of the week, the Lord's day (Acts 20:7). We also know that this elect group is delivered up to synagogues (Mark 13:9). We do not meet in synagogues. We are members of His Church (Acts 2:47), and furthermore, these synagogues are in the vicinity of Jerusalem (Luke 21:24).

And then there is the idea of the wolf and the lamb living in peace and harmony? Regardless of those who scoff at this phenomenon, this is exactly how the two animals will relate to each other during the Millennium.

And then there is the idea of the wolf and the lamb living in peace and harmony? Regardless of those who scoff at this phenomenon, this is exactly how the two animals will relate to each other during the Millennium. However, again, controversy arises when some theologians argue that this is only symbolic. They say that this idea of a wolf and a lamb coexisting in peace is tantamount to the remarkable change that took place as the vicious persecutor Saul of Tarsus, a ravaging and destroying wolf, became a lamb through conversion. This is how ridiculously some scholars do away with the literalness of God's Holy Word. We might say to these theologians, "Nice try." But it simply does not hold water with the rest of the counsel of Scripture. Instead, it is symbolization to the extreme.

The easiest—and most correct—way to study God's Word is to accept it as literally true. This can even be said of the book of Revelation. We must regard this otherwise difficult book as literal unless God tells us to take some symbol in it figuratively. In my analysis of every verse in the book of Revelation in my volume entitled, *Revelation*

Revealed, I prove that every symbol can be literally explained through scores of Old Testament texts. Thus, we can understand and trust this Holy Book. Revelation 1:3 states, "Blessed is he that readeth, and they that hear the words of this prophecy, and keep those things which are written therein." Would we not have a foolish God if He promises a special blessing to the readers, the hearers, and the keepers of what they hear and read if they could not understand it?

I want to close this section concerning the Millennial *controversy* by referring to one more challenge often offered to criticize the actual existence of the thousand-year earthly reign of Jesus Christ. Unfortunately, some Bible scholars rely on obscure passages of Scripture to hide the truth. Many also claim that the message of the Old Testament is exalted over the teaching of the New. This is patently false. The Scriptures of both Old and New Testaments are God's Word to the fullest and must be honored. No passage contradicts any other. In fact, 2 Timothy 3:16 talks exclusively about the Old Testament as does 2 Peter 1:12-21. For example, Jesus made the statement in Matthew 4:4 that "Man shall not live by bread alone, but by every word that proceedeth out of the mouth of God." That verse appears in the New Testament. But what was Jesus quoting? That's right— the Old Testament. There is no contradiction. As part of my research, I've read seventy-two different volumes on this subject by seventy-two of the world's greatest theological scholars. In poring over this exhaustive array of material, it became more than obvious that literally hundreds of verses support the pre-Millennium point of view, not just one isolated text, as the detractors say when referring to Revelation 20:4, "They lived and reigned with Christ a thousand years." However, even if there *were* only one text supporting the pre-Millennial position, and there are scores of verses substantiating this viewpoint, it would cause no problem. Why? Because if God said it once, that is enough. Entire denominations have been founded on a single verse, and the teaching for some practices within these denominational groups cannot even be located in God's Word. They are built upon a foundation of sand because of man-made interpretations. So if there were only one text, why would we not believe it to be literally true?

> In poring over this exhaustive array of material, it becomes more than obvious that literally hundreds of verses support the pre-Millennium point of view, not just one isolated text, as the detractors say.

TIME LINE FROM CHRIST TO THE MILLENNIUM

To this point, we have laid the foundation for the validity of Christ's physical return to earth to rule for a thousand years. Now, in the chapters that lie ahead, we will witness what happens when Christ returns and what life will be like on this earth during this incredible, peaceful period of history. We observe our initial panoramic view of this event as we study Revelation chapter 19 where the marriage of the Lamb occurs in verse 7. This is the union of Christ and His Bride, also called the Church. This ceremony takes place in heaven. Immediately after the wedding we see the King returning (verse 11), with His Bride for a thousand-year honeymoon (verse 14), when He returns as King (verse 16). But as He descends, earthly armies, in verse 19, attempt to keep Him from setting up His kingdom. Though they are formidable forces, they are immediately defeated, and their leaders, primarily the beast and the false prophet, are cast into the lake of fire (Revelation 19:20). Next, the Lord binds Satan and throws him into the bottomless pit for a thousand years (Revelation 20:1-3). At this point in time, the resurrection of Tribulation saints takes place (verse 4)—as well as the raising of the Old Testament Jewish believers (Daniel 12:2). After raising the Old Testament and Tribulation saints, Jesus sets up His kingdom for one thousand years of peace, such as the world has never known, and calls all the resurrected guests and living believers who survive the judgment of Matthew 25:31-46 to the greatest and largest event in history, the Marriage Supper of the Lamb, in fulfillment of John 3:29 and Revelation 19:9. Sadly, however, Satan rises from the bottomless pit after a thousand years and instantaneously leads millions upon millions against Christ. The Lord, at this juncture, determines that judgment is necessary and casts the devil and his demons into the lake of fire (Revelation 20:10). At this point the lost, including the rebels who turned against Christ at the conclusion of the Millennium along with the millions of sinners raised from the dead from past centuries, are eternally judged (Revelation 20:11-15).

> There can be no kingdom without the king being present. If this doesn't happen, millions of Christians for hundreds of years have wasted their time and prayers by obeying Jesus who taught his disciples to pray, thy kingdom come, thy will be done, on earth as it is in heaven. Christ's eternal kingdom will be realized on this planet as well as in heaven.
>
> —DR. J. VERNON MCGEE

My friend Dr. J. Vernon McGee, now present with the Lord, once made a statement that has stayed with me during all my years of ministry. He wrote: "There can be no kingdom without the king being present. If this doesn't happen, millions of Christians for hundreds of years have wasted their time and prayers by obeying Jesus who taught his disciples to pray, thy kingdom come, thy will be done, on earth as it is in heaven. Christ's eternal kingdom will be realized on this planet as well as in heaven."

So simple, and yet so profound. Of the millions of words that have been written about the Millennium, Dr. McGee has perhaps said it best. I encourage you to study this issue for yourself. Here is the chronological sequence: Jesus Christ came the first time and offered Himself as Israel's King. John the Baptist, 2,000 years ago, also proclaimed that the kingdom of heaven was at hand (Matthew 3:2). But something happened. In John 1:11 we read, "He came unto his own [the Jewish people], and his own received him not." The would-be king had few subjects and, to the chagrin of His would-be followers, He had only the bare shred of an earthly kingdom. Hardly anything at all. So Christ, commenting on the attitude of His people in that day, said, "O Jerusalem, Jerusalem, thou that killest the prophets, and stonest them which are sent unto thee, how often would I have gathered thy children together, even as a hen gathereth her chickens under her wings, and ye would not!" (Matthew 23:37). His would-be subjects rejected their King. This happened as He headed for Calvary's cross (John 19:15), as the hateful crowds shouted, "Away with him, away with him, crucify him." However, above the cross were written the words, "Jesus, the king of the Jews."

His kingdom was rejected and here's why: The people did not, in Old Testament times, understand 1 Peter 1:11 concerning "the sufferings of Christ, and the glory that should follow." They were unaware that there would be two appearances. The people of Jesus' day looked for a king who would rise up with a rod of iron and rule the world, take away their shackles, and set them free from the terrible bondage of Rome. What a disappointment it was for them to see the gentle Lamb of God spiked to a rugged, wooden cross. Their misunderstanding of Scripture caused their rejection. Nevertheless, this was all in God's plan. His rejection was simply a prelude to what happens when the King returns and is accepted—a day that fast approaches and may occur during our lifetime.

How do we know the King will soon appear? God's Word states that when Jerusalem is captured by the Jews (Luke 21:24), "there shall be signs in the sun, and in the moon, and in the stars; and upon the earth distress of nations, with perplexity; the sea and the waves roaring; men's hearts failing them for fear, and for looking after those things which are coming on the earth: for the powers of heaven shall be shaken. And then shall they see the Son of man coming in a cloud with power and great glory" (Luke 21:25-27). This prophecy uttered by Jesus refers to nothing else but His kingdom arriving upon earth. Soon He will descend from heaven, appearing on the Mount of Olives, even as the nations of the world are converged against Jerusalem and against Christ for the scourge of Armageddon (Psalm 2:1; Zechariah 14:4-16; Revelation 19:19). After this horrendous battle, millions upon millions of people—probably three billion—from all nations will still be alive. Then, as judgment begins in this very location upon Christ's return, millions who survived Armageddon will be judged and will suffer eternal loss (Matthew 25:41, 46). The remainder will be invited to become participants in Christ's glorious kingdom on earth for a thousand years (Matthew 25:34), to worship the King at Jerusalem for centuries to come (Zechariah 14:16). Nothing symbolic here. No need to *spiritualize* away the truth of Scripture. The events I have just described will happen as sure as clockwork, and the time for their unfolding is upon us. Not to accept these facts literally is to do a disservice to the Word of God.

"For as the lightning cometh out of the east, and shineth even unto the west; so shall also the coming of the Son of man be."
(Matthew 24:27)

CHAPTER 3

THE GLORIOUS SECOND COMING OF JESUS CHRIST

One of the truly great Bible prophecy teachers of our generation, Dr. John F. Walvoord, has never flinched from expressing his deep belief in the importance of teaching and preaching the Millennial doctrine. I could quote him repeatedly on his insistence that the biblical teaching on the subject of the Millennium must be an intricate part of anyone's understanding of the whole counsel of Scripture. He has always ably put his thoughts into an easy-to-understand historical context, and continually reminded the reader that the so-called Millennium controversy is nothing new, but has existed since the third century—a conflict we have already referred to in the first two chapters. Today, more than at any time in our history, questions are being asked about a future Millennium on earth. I feel it is important that we hear directly from the pen of

Dr. Walvoord. Here are his words, written in the late 1950s, but ever fresh today.

The question has been raised whether the discussion of the millennium doctrine is in itself important and worthy of the consideration of the scholarly world. There remains today a tendency to dismiss the whole subject as belonging to another era and as being foreign to intellectual studies of our day. . . . On the other hand, the continued production of books on the subject points to a growing realization that the issue is more important than appears on the surface. If premillennialism is only a dispute about what will happen in the future age which is quite removed from present issues, that is one thing. If, however, premillennialism is a system of interpretation which involves the meaning and significance of the entire Bible, defines the meaning and course of the present age, determines the present purpose of God, and gives both material and method to theology, that is something else. It is the growing realization that premillennialism is more than a dispute about Revelation 20 that has precipitated the extended arguments on the issue in our day. For the first time it seems to be commonly recognized that premillennial theology has become a system of theology, not an alternative view of its eschatology which is unrelated to theology as a whole.[1]

Thank you, Dr. Walvoord, not only for your bold evangelical leadership during an era when your interpretation of biblical prophecy was not always appreciated, but also for your continual guidance as we, in our era, attempt to "rightly divide the word of truth" and be faithful to God's Word.

Earlier we spoke briefly of the Rapture of the Church of Jesus Christ, that momentous time in history when we who believe will be removed before the Tribulation period begins, only to return with Christ during His Second Coming, known as the revelation *and the beginning of the thousand-year earthly reign of our Lord Jesus Christ*. Based on the thousands of questions Rexella and I receive regularly from our television viewers regarding these two pivotal events, I think it is important to clarify the difference between the two. In Revelation 4:1, we discover the Rapture—the "snatching away"—when Jesus says, "Come up hither." Seven years later, Revelation 19:11, we experience His revealing to the world. John says, "I saw heaven opened, and behold a white horse; and he that sat upon him was called Faithful and True." Jesus makes His exit from heaven to earth, and the armies in heaven follow Him (verse 14). At that precise moment, He comes as King of kings and Lord of lords (verse 16). In Revelation 4:1, He comes as Savior. In Revelation 19:16, He comes as King. In Revelation 4, He comes before the horrendous twenty-one judgments listed in chapters 6 through 18 begin. In chapter 19, He returns with His saints who have missed that terrible, catastrophic time in history. In this final book of the Bible, Jesus reveals Himself to the entire world instantaneously: "Behold, he cometh with clouds; and every eye shall see him" (Revelation 1:7). Because He reveals himself globally, we call it His "revealing," or the larger term, His "revelation." This revelation, then, is the opening phase of the coming Millennium, setting in motion on planet earth events that bring every aspect of the social, spiritual, and physical environment eventually into a serenity never before experienced by mortal man.

> Millions still remain unconvinced that we are coming to a new threshold of existence as we know it where the wolf *will* lie down with the lamb and the world will experience universal peace.

THE SIGNS OF HIS COMING

Despite the many signs that indicate Christ's second appearing is near, millions still remain unconvinced that we are coming to a new threshold of existence where the wolf *will* lie down with the lamb and the world will experience universal peace (Isaiah 2:4 and 11:6). In an attempt to persuade skeptics to open their minds and hearts to objective proof, let me present a thumbnail sketch of what has happened prophetically in our world that demonstrates we are closer than ever to the greatest moment in time—Christ's return. The signs of Jesus' Second Coming are many and are found in both the Old and New Testaments. I encourage you to review the verses for each of the following indicators of Christ's return:

1. Airplanes (Isaiah 31:5)

2. Horseless carriages or automobiles (Nahum 2:3-4)

3. The desert blossoming as a rose (Isaiah 35:1)

4. The alignment of a ten-nation Western confederacy (Daniel 2 and 7)

5. The knowledge explosion (Daniel 12:4)

6. Great increases in travel (Daniel 12:4)

7. False Christs and false prophets (Matthew 24:5, 11, 24; and 2 Peter 2:1)

8. Wars and rumors of wars (Mark 13:7)

9. Famines (Matthew 24:7)

10. Earthquakes in divers places (Mark 13:8)

11. Pestilences (Luke 21:11)

12. Iniquity abounding (Matthew 24:12)

13. The gospel of the kingdom preached in all the world (Matthew 24:14)

14. Signs in the sun, moon, and stars (Luke 17:26-30 and 21:25-27)

15. The introduction of evil spirits, cults, and apostates (1 Timothy 4:1-2)

16. The nineteen signs of 2 Timothy 3:1-5

17. The hoarding of gold and silver and its final demise (James 5:1-3 and Revelation 18:17)

18. False prophets denying the deity of Christ (2 Peter 2:1-3)

19. Scoffers mocking the Second Coming of Christ (2 Peter 3:3-4)

20. The invention of the atom bomb (2 Peter 3:10)

21. Lethargy and indifference among God's people (Revelation 3:15-17)

The judgments described in the book of Revelation 6–18 are usually identical to the signs found in Matthew 24, Mark 13, and Luke 17 and 21. Many of these events have already taken place; others are in the initial stages of fulfillment. Because of the authenticity of God's Word, I encourage you to read your Bible as never before and to work diligently at becoming a serious, astute observer of current events.

And I saw heaven opened, and behold a white horse; and he that sat upon him was called Faithful and True, and in righteousness he doth judge and make war (Revelation 19:11).

CHRIST'S DESCENT FROM HEAVEN

Jesus describes His return to earth in Matthew 24:27-31:

> "For as the lightning cometh out of the east, and shineth even unto the west; so shall also the coming of the Son of man be. For wheresoever the carcase is, there will the eagles be gathered together. Immediately after the tribulation of those days shall the sun be darkened, and the moon shall not give her light, and the stars shall fall from heaven, and the powers of the heavens shall be shaken: And then shall appear the sign of the Son of man in heaven: and then shall all the tribes of the earth mourn, and they shall see the Son of man coming in the clouds of heaven with power and great glory. And he shall send his angels with a great sound of a trumpet, and they shall gather together his elect from the four winds, from one end of heaven to the other."

This, my friend, is one of the most graphic expressions in the Bible regarding the Second Coming of Christ. Another key passage that relates to this event is found in Revelation 19:11-16. In this passage, John describes our Lord as coming out of heaven riding a white horse—as a warrior. Here is how John describes this event:

And I saw heaven opened, and behold a white horse; and he that sat upon him was called Faithful and True, and in righteousness he doth judge and make war. His eyes were as a flame of fire, and on his head were many crowns; and he had a name written, that no man knew, but he himself. And he was clothed with a vesture dipped in blood: and his name is called The Word of God. And the armies which were in heaven followed him upon white horses, clothed in fine linen, white and clean. And out of his mouth goeth a sharp sword, that with it he should smite the nations: and he shall rule them with a rod of iron: and he treadeth the winepress of the fierceness and wrath of Almighty God. And he hath on his vesture and on his thigh a name written, KING OF KINGS, AND LORD OF LORDS.

Hollywood may think *it* knows how to write a heart-stopping opening to a blockbuster movie, but nothing ever penned or created will compare to the opening moments of the Millennium, an event that will be observed internationally as Christ comes to earth in a brilliant display of divine glory, adorned with many crowns. In Revelation 19:12, the Greek word *diadema,* translated "crowns," means a white linen band encircling the brow, signifying royalty. And royalty Christ is and ever shall be. In the Millennial Kingdom, soon to begin, these crowns represent Christ's dominion over all the kings and rulers of the earth, who still maintain their local governments under the supervision of the glorious King of kings and Lord of lords.

> Hollywood may think it knows how to write a heart-stopping opening to a blockbuster movie, but nothing ever penned or created will compare to the opening moments of the Millennium.

At this point I want you to use your most vivid imagination for a moment as you observe the gates of heaven opened as the King of kings readies himself for His descent to our planet. Do you see His vast armies following Him with their enormous power? Do you also see the holy angels and saints, from the time of earth's first man, Adam, to the Rapture, all tailored in their most resplendent robes, eagerly following their Lord back to earth? The energy of a million earthly dynamos (generators), run by the most powerful fuel that science can develop, will pale in comparison to the sheer raw power assembled in the courts of heaven on that fateful day as Jesus returns with myriads of angels and saints to smite the nations and rule them with a rod of iron. And why is He coming with such enormous force? Because only the personal presence of our Lord and Savior Jesus Christ, and His saints who rule and reign with Him, will provide the draconian measures necessary to solve the problems that continue to fester on earth. His divine and majestic presence will be the cure for what ails humankind as He comes with force to enact His will and to stop mankind from destroying the earth and one another (Revelation 11:18).

HEAVENLY CITIZENS JOIN TOGETHER FOR A GREAT EARTHLY CELEBRATION

And who are those saints who live and reign with Christ during the Millennium? The Bible makes it clear that three classes of people will appear with our Lord. One will be the returning saints. Jude verse 14 says, "And Enoch also, the seventh from Adam, prophesied of these, saying, Behold, the Lord cometh with ten thousands of his saints." Revelation 19:14 adds: "And the armies which were in heaven followed him upon white horses, clothed in fine linen, white and clean." What an incredible sight that will be to see the returning saints, yes, the armies of heaven, making their descent to earth. Group two will be made up of resurrected Old Testament saints. Daniel 12:1-2 reads:

And at that time shall Michael stand up, the great prince which standeth for the children of thy people: and there shall be a time of trouble, such as never was since there was a nation even to that same time: and at that time thy people shall be delivered, every one that shall be found written in the book. And many of them that sleep in the dust of the earth shall awake, some to everlasting life, and some to shame and everlasting contempt.

Group three will be the host of resurrected saints of the Tribulation hour. Revelation 20:4 tells us, "And I saw thrones, and they sat upon them, and judgment was given unto them: and I saw the souls of them that were beheaded for the witness of Jesus, and for the word of God, and which had not worshipped the beast, neither his image, neither had received his mark upon their foreheads, or in their hands; and they lived and reigned with Christ a thousand years."

> He will come with the blinding fury of a lightning flash, set in stark relief against a darkened sun, an opaque moon, and what will appear to be an enormous veil that shields the light from the stars.

Yes, my friend, the Second Coming of our Lord will be like no other event in the history of the world. How spectacular will Christ's return be? Let's look at what Jesus Himself said of the event in Matthew 24:27, "As the lightning cometh out of the east, and shineth even unto the west, so shall also the coming of the Son of man be." No wonder *every eye shall see Him!* Some scholars speculate that the third heaven of 2 Corinthians 12:2 is some 2,932,848,000,000,000,000,000 miles from earth—well beyond the pale of our universe. Yet, our Lord will come to earth with the speed of lightning. He will descend from heaven with the blinding fury of a lightning flash, set in stark relief against a darkened sun, an opaque moon, and what will appear to be an enormous veil that shields the light from the stars (Matthew 24:27).

WITH BRUTAL, SEISMIC FORCE . . .

Would you not agree that we have a powerful, awesome God to worship? So powerful that even the stars (*aster* in Greek, which also means "shooting stars" or "meteors") obey His commands and demonstrate their celestial fireworks for the entire world to see. There will literally be a storm of meteors covering the earth as if it were a rain shower—but descending with seismic, brutal force. Again, let your imagination do its work. Jesus comes to earth with His angels and saints of all ages past in one tremendous blaze of power and glory: to a darkened earth shattered with the force of meteors, out of a blackened sky (Revelation 6:12). Our Lord describes this as a "sign" of the Son of man. In Greek, the word for "sign" is *semeion,* meaning a *miracle* whose purpose is to declare the divine source of the message *delivered by the one performing the miracle.* And what is the miracle here? *It is a spectacular, never-before-seen, earth-shattering event whose merciful objective is to prove to earth dwellers that the One who comes from heaven is indeed the Son of God, the One who is to be received with joy and thanksgiving.*

> With meteors showering their land and darkness settling on the earth and heavenly armies rising up to do battle against evil, one could safely assume that few earth dwellers will be saying to their neighbors, "Have a nice day."

But will the inhabitants of earth be joyful? Hardly. Revelation 1:7 tells us, "Behold, he cometh with clouds; and every eye shall see him, and they also which pierced him: and all kindreds of the earth shall wail because of him." So, they will not rejoice. With meteors showering their land and darkness settling on the earth and heavenly armies rising up to do battle against evil, one could safely assume that few earth dwellers will be saying to their neighbors, "Have a nice day." It will not seem like a pleasant day at all. We are told that the earth dwellers will mourn. They will remember how their forefathers rejected Him centuries before when He offered Himself as their King. The Greek word for "mourn" is so descriptive. *Kopto* means "to beat one's breast in grief." People will wail tears of anger, grief, resentment, and frustration. However, peace soon will take over as swords are beaten and battered into plowshares, the earth is restored, and the deserts blossom as a rose (Isaiah 2:4; Micah 4:3; and Isaiah 35:1).

How soon are we to expect the day of Christ's appearing on earth? Prophetic signs inform us that the time is closer today than it was yesterday. We are living in momentous times. The rapid movement of current events substantiates incontrovertibly the truths of the Word of God and are enough to strike awe into the hearts of those looking for His appearing. When He comes, He *will* reign in power, might, glory, and victory. My prayer for you is—despite the terror and uncertainty of the days in which we live—that you will remain strong and resilient, recognizing constantly that our Lord will win the final battle and that He, at all times, has you under His protective wings. Let the encouraging words of Jesus in John 14:27 comfort and sustain you, "Peace I leave with you, my peace I give unto you: not as the world giveth, give I unto you. Let not your heart be troubled, neither let it be afraid."

Then shall the LORD go forth, and fight against those nations, as when he fought in the day of battle. And his feet shall stand in that day upon the mount of Olives, which is before Jerusalem on the east, and the mount of Olives shall cleave in the midst thereof toward the east and toward the west, and there shall be a very great valley; and half of the mountain shall remove toward the north, and half of it toward the south. And ye shall flee to the valley of the mountains; for the valley of the mountains shall reach unto Azal: yea, ye shall flee, like as ye fled from before the earthquake in the days of Uzziah king of Judah: and the LORD my God shall come, and all the saints with thee.
(Zechariah 14:3-5)

CHAPTER 4

THE GREAT
CAMPAIGN

❧

The Word of God makes it patently clear that the event to usher in the Millennium will be when our Lord's feet touch down on the Mount of Olives. Zechariah 14:3-4 states: "Then shall the LORD go forth, and fight against those nations, as when he fought in the day of battle. And his feet shall stand in that day upon the mount of Olives, which is before Jerusalem on the east, and the mount of Olives shall cleave in the midst thereof toward the east and toward the west, and there shall be a very great valley; and half of the mountain shall remove toward the north, and half of it toward the south." You will recall that Christ ascended into heaven from that same mount. Acts 1:8-11 tells us,

> "But ye shall receive power, after that the Holy Ghost
> is come upon you: and ye shall be witnesses unto me
> both in Jerusalem, and in all Judaea, and in Samaria,

and unto the uttermost part of the earth." And when he had spoken these things, while they beheld, he was taken up; and a cloud received him out of their sight. And while they looked stedfastly toward heaven as he went up, behold, two men stood by them in white apparel; Which also said, Ye men of Galilee, why stand ye gazing up into heaven? this same Jesus, which is taken up from you into heaven, shall so come in like manner [to the same location] as ye have seen him go into heaven.

Now, these many centuries later, we finally come to that long awaited moment in history when Jesus' own promise to His Church is fulfilled. The Rapture has come and gone, the Tribulation upon earth has accomplished its goal, and now our Lord returns in power, majesty, and glory, even as the angels promised (Acts 1:11).

> In a flash, our Savior's contact with terra firma will initiate an earthquake unlike any temblor California or the beleaguered nations of Latin America have ever experienced.

AN EARTHQUAKE LIKE NO OTHER

And what will be the result of Christ's visible return to earth? In a flash, our Savior's contact with terra firma will initiate an earthquake unlike any temblor California or the beleaguered nations of Latin America have ever experienced. Its epicenter will be the Mount of Olives, and it will rattle the earth with such lethal force that it will break the mountains in two halves. As the shock waves of this monstrous quake are felt, the violence will increase. Zechariah 14:4 describes the scene: "And his feet shall stand in that day upon the mount of Olives, which is before Jerusalem on the east, and the mount of Olives shall cleave in the midst thereof toward the east and toward the west, and there shall be a very great valley; and half of the mountain shall remove toward the north, and half of it toward the south." The correlating text in the New Testament is Revelation 16:18, "And there were voices, and thunders, and lightnings; and there was a great earthquake, such as was not since men were upon the earth, so mighty an earthquake, and so great."

> If earth's people ever doubted the power and presence of God in the past, they will never again question His majesty as He makes His grand entrance to initiate the Millennial Kingdom with a rod of iron.

Do I now have your attention? This is no puny, ordinary 5.5 earthquake. It is not even a 7.0. The intensity of this earth shaker goes beyond what the Richter scale has the ability to measure. If earth's people ever doubted the power and presence of God in the past, they will never

again question His majesty as He makes His grand
entrance to initiate the Millennial Kingdom with a rod of
iron.

THE BATTLE OF ARMAGEDDON

Several years ago when my wife, Rexella, and I were
in the Holy Land making programs for television, one of
our nationwide releases was scheduled to be on the subject of Armageddon. As Rexella maneuvered her way
through the crowded streets of Jerusalem with our television crew, she repeatedly asked the question, "What does
the term *Armageddon* mean to you?" Virtually every person she spoke with responded by saying, "Why, it's the
end of the world." How wrong millions upon millions are
as they think this and give this answer. Why?
Armageddon is not a sad ending but, instead, a glorious
beginning as Christ returns to earth to halt mankind's
destruction of one another and then to set up His
Millennial reign of peace, love, joy, and security. Why,
then, does so much confusion reign today, and how did
the "end of the world" philosophy begin? Let me give you
some historical background from Jewish tradition on this
important subject. The rabbis of old taught that the
Messiah would one day appear to set up his rule and to
reign upon the earth. (Psalm 2:6; Isaiah 9:6-7; Zechariah
14:4, 16, as well as in numerous other Old Testament
texts.) The Church Fathers continued this scriptural

teaching for the first 400 years of Christendom. In fact, in the year A.D. 325, 318 bishops of the Church met in session in Nicaea and reaffirmed the one-thousand-year reign of Christ—our Lord's Millennial Kingdom. So far, so good.

However, in the next century, an anti-Jewish atmosphere developed in Christendom, and Origen, whom Pope John Paul II called a heretic in his book *Crossing the Threshold of Hope*, and his compatriot Ambrose influenced St. Augustine to change the teaching—a heresy we alluded to earlier. From the council of Ephesus in A.D. 431 onward, the idea of a "one-thousand-year reign" of Christ was substituted for the "end of the world" doomsday error that, the dissidents said, would take place at the battle of Armageddon. This anti-Semitic teaching has been perpetuated throughout the past fifteen centuries and doctrinally is seriously and drastically wrong. Instead, Armageddon, as already mentioned, is not a sad ending but rather a glorious beginning because Christ's appearing and reign ends mankind's bias and hatred for one thousand years (Revelation 11:18b). Then, following the Millennial rule of Christ, our Lord is recommissioned and His earthly rule continues forever and ever in a world that will never end (Isaiah 45:17 and Ephesians 3:21).

Concerning the Armageddon campaign, some of Judaism's most renowned rabbis and scholars have spoken with one voice, stating in the *Midrash Tehellium* that three different attacks occur against Jerusalem during the

Armageddon campaign. (This note of clarification: While it is often thought that the battle of Armageddon is an isolated event that takes place prior to the Second Coming of Christ to earth, we now know this is not the case. Instead of a single *battle,* this gigantic war of wars must be seen as a *campaign* that extends over the last half [or three-and-one-half years] of the Tribulation period. The Greek word *polemos,* translated "battle" in Revelation 16:14, means "a campaign.") Thus, this triad of military advances mentioned by these scholars in the forty-two-month war includes Russia—*This is the first military wave* of the three-pronged Armageddon campaign when the king of the south (Egypt and her Arab Federation) and the king of the north (Russia) begin their pincer movement against Israel (Daniel 11:40; Ezekiel 38:5-6; and Psalm 83:4). Ezekiel 38:16 says, "And thou shalt come up against my people of Israel, as a cloud to cover the land; it shall be in the latter days, and I will bring thee against my land, that the heathen may know me, when I shall be sanctified in thee, O Gog, before their eyes." Once Russia has made her move, the Antichrist furiously enters the *glorious land,* Israel (Daniel 11:41).

Some of Judaism's most renowned rabbis have spoken with one voice, saying that there will be three different attacks against Jerusalem at the time of the Messiah's appearing.

Immediately the Antichrist situates himself in Jerusalem—in the Jewish temple at the midpoint of the Tribulation hour—the second three and one-half years, calling himself God. Since he knows that he has but a short time to do his global mischief while incarnated by Satan, he spews forth wrath and hatred. When he hears that Russia and the Arab Federation are invading the region, he moves at breakneck speed and puts an end to the militaristic activity of Russia, Egypt, and their allies. The European Union has taken a position in the conflict under the infamous Antichrist, who subdues and drives back the first wave of Russian and Arab invaders. At this point, Russia has fled to Siberia, as we read in Joel 2:20, "But I will remove far off from you the northern army, and will drive him into a land barren and desolate, with his face toward the east sea, and his hinder part toward the utmost sea, and his stink shall come up, and his ill savour shall come up, because he hath done great things."

> The Antichrist is now on a bloody rampage. He's heard that great hoards of oriental armies are moving down into the region to do battle, accompanied by the leftover ragtag army of Russia that had previously been pushed back to Siberia.

Now the *second movement* of troops is about to move into the Middle East against Israel. Daniel 11:44 states, "Tidings out of the east and out of the north shall trouble him: therefore he shall go forth with great fury to destroy." The Antichrist is now on a bloody rampage. He's heard that great hoards of oriental armies are moving down into the region to do battle, accompanied by the leftover ragtag army of Russia that had previously been pushed back to Siberia. This frustrates him as he wonders how he will muster the troops to fend off 200 million soldiers (Revelation 9:16). Overwhelmed and fearful, he wonders how he will be able to maintain an adequate power base to defend himself. During the first wave, the Antichrist is killed by Gog of Russia (Daniel 11:45). However, he suddenly comes back to life, duplicating the resurrection of Jesus Christ—something no one in history has ever done (Revelation 13:3). He flaunts this demonic miracle and uses it to position himself as a god among men, reestablishing himself when he needs it most—when his reputation and strength are on the line. Because of his miraculous resurrection, the entire world falls at his feet, "And all that dwell upon the earth shall worship him, whose names are not written in the book of life of the Lamb slain from the foundation of the world" (Revelation 13:8).

Now at this point China and the remnants of Russia's fallen army join in the fray for the second wave of the Armageddon campaign, as 200 million soldiers move against Israel—not a difficult assignment for a nation that, in the next decade, *will boast a population of more than 1.4 billion people.* Remember when John predicted an army of 200 million approximately 2,000 years ago? The world's entire population wasn't that large then, so God's spirit undoubtedly had our day in mind when He inspired John to use this astronomical figure. Let's continue. This gigantic army marches out of the Orient downward across the areas of Iraq and Syria. Revelation 16:12 says, "The sixth angel poured out his vial upon the great river Euphrates; and the water thereof was dried up, that the way of the kings of the east might be prepared." This second wave of horrendous military power eliminates one-third of earth's inhabitants (Revelation 9:18). In spite of this colossal power, China and the left-over armies of Russia from the first invasion are also defeated.

> The location of the campaign, the hill of Megiddo, is located west of the Jordan River—about ten miles south of Nazareth and fifteen miles inland from the Mediterranean. It has already played an enormous role in Israel's many historic battles.

Finally, in the *third and closing scene* of the Armageddon campaign, the Antichrist and his armies battle Christ in what becomes the war to end all wars. Armageddon or Har-Megeddo is the gathering place (Revelation 16:16). A bit of history regarding this place: The location of the campaign, the hill of Megiddo, is located west of the Jordan River—about ten miles south of Nazareth and fifteen miles inland from the Mediterranean. It has already played an enormous role in Israel's many historic battles. There Deborah and Barak defeated the Canaanites (Judges 4 and 5); it was on the hill of Megiddo that Gideon was victorious over the Midianites (Judges 7); there Saul was killed in the battle with the Philistines (1 Samuel 31:8). These are only a few of the historical events that took place there.

Scholars remind us that Megiddo (located in the plain of Esdraelon) has been a chosen place for encampment in virtually every contest carried on in Palestine from the days of Nabuchodonozor, king of Assyria, to the disastrous march of Napoleon Bonaparte from Egypt into Syria. Jews, Gentiles, Saracens, Christian crusaders, Persians, Turks, and warriors from every nation have pitched their tents on the plains of Esdraelon. It is from this place that the armies will march to the valley of Jehoshaphat (Joel 3:2). Then the third and final attack will occur as all nations gather against Jerusalem to battle (Zechariah 14:2).

The Antichrist will do everything in his power during his final forty-two months to pour out venom on his enemies, including the ultimate blasphemy against Christ by saying, "I will keep the King of kings from coming to power." Egotistically, he believes he will also be victorious against the Lord of Hosts. How dead wrong he will be. Revelation 19:19 sets the stage for this apocalyptic event and depicts the Antichrist's frivolous plans stating: "I saw the beast, and the kings of the earth, and their armies, gathered together to make war against him that sat on the horse, and against his army."

In Revelation 19:11, Christ appears on a white horse to rule as King of kings and Lord of lords. But stubborn and rebellious to the end, the Antichrist insists any enemy, including Christ, will never defeat him. However, this time he is wrong, because Christ destroys him with the brightness of His coming (2 Thessalonians 2:8). Christ then takes the global dictator—along with the false prophet who headed up the world church— and casts them both into a lake of fire (Revelation 19:20). A thousand years later, when Satan is thrown into that same lake of fire, the beast and the false prophet still exist, suffering the torment of hell forever and ever (Revelation 20:10).

As we summarize the campaign of Armageddon, we see several results: (1) the vast armies under the leader of the south wiped out during the battle; (2) the armies of the north eliminated by the Lord; (3) the armies of the beast destroyed by the Lord at His Second Coming; (4) the beast and the false prophet thrown forever into the lake of fire (Revelation 19:20); and (5) Satan bound (Revelation 20:2). With these events behind Him, the Lord of lords puts down every hostile force that would dare challenge His right to rule as Messiah over all the earth.

Armageddon is not a sad ending at all, but a glorious beginning under the rulership of the Lord Jesus Christ in which our Lord will put down all earth's angry forces as He creates a thousand years of utopian peace upon earth.

When will these momentous events take place? In the latter years and the latter days (Ezekiel 38:8, 16). The ancient Jewish writing—*Avodah Zara* 3B states, "The war of Gog and Magog [Russia] will be one of the key events to usher in the Messianic Era [Christ's return]." The revered *Jerusalem Targum* adds: "At the end of days, Gog and Magog shall march against Jerusalem, but perish by the hand of Messiah [Christ]." I agree because 2 Thessalonians 2:8 teaches that our Lord will destroy the wicked one with the brightness of His coming. As Christ returns to earth in majesty and great glory to rule and reign for one thousand years, Isaiah 2:4 becomes a reality: "They shall beat their swords into plowshares, and their spears into pruninghooks . . . neither shall they learn war any more." How long will all this last? Isaiah 9:7 says, "Of the increase of his government and peace there shall be no end, . . . henceforth even for ever . . ." So I repeat, Armageddon is not a sad ending at all, but a glorious beginning under the rulership of our Lord Jesus Christ who puts down all earth's angry forces as He creates a thousand years of utopian peace upon earth.

THE EARTH IN RUINS

With his once wide-flung kingdom now lying in ruins—Europe devastated by the quake to end all quakes, the Mediterranean a virtual sea of blood, earth's inhabitants inflicted by sores and an inability to endure the heat from the sun, people forced to drink water that has turned to blood—the Antichrist realizes he has finally met his match. As it turns out, he is not god after all, but rather a frail, insignificant man who had spent too much time poring over and believing his own press releases. It was all a setup! Now it's over. He's doomed eternally, and with his demise, the Lord of Glory sets up earth's golden age and gives all humanity one more glorious opportunity to live life to its fullest.

Beloved, believe not every spirit, but try the spirits whether they are of God: because many false prophets are gone out into the world.
(1 John 4:1)

CHAPTER 5

THE MILLENNIAL
JUDGMENT

s I sat down to write this chapter, my eye caught
a sizable stack of letters lying on the corner of my
desk, letters with literally scores of sincere questions about the latter days, the Tribulation period, the final
judgments, and the Millennium. As I leafed through the
correspondence, person after person asked, "Jack, what
really are the signs that we are facing the greatest event in
history—Christ's return?" Such questions sent to Rexella
and me by our television viewers are so important that I
think, before beginning our dialogue on the judgment that
occurs at Christ's Second Coming, I would like to share
some additional detail on why I know beyond doubt that
the clock of time is ticking faster then ever, reminding us
that we are on a collision course with history. I trust that
what I have to say will excite, encourage, and help prepare
you for the rest of this chapter and book. As you know,
when the disciples questioned Jesus directly about His

final return to earth as King of kings and Lord of lords, they received a complete rundown, an exposé, if you like, on latter-day events. Any fair examination of Jesus' words is sure to lead the reader to one conclusion—that we are living in the very times Jesus described. The first sign Jesus mentioned is the rise of false Christs and false prophets. He said, "For many shall come in my name, saying, I am Christ; and shall deceive many" (Matthew 24:5). Presently, we live in an age in which self-proclaimed messiahs abound. We are told in 1 John 4:1, "Beloved, believe not every spirit, but try the spirits whether they are of God: because many false prophets are gone out into the world." How can we discern the legitimate spirits from the illegitimate? The answer comes in the next two verses, "Hereby know ye the Spirit of God: Every spirit that confesseth that Jesus Christ is come in the flesh is of God: And every spirit that confesseth not that Jesus Christ is come in the flesh is not of God: and this is that spirit of antichrist, whereof ye have heard that it should come; and even now already is it in the world." This spirit of Antichrist mentioned in 1 John 2:18, 22; 4:3; and 2 John 1:7 has to do with the denial of Christ's deity.

> The planet will be consumed in violence, revolution, upheaval, and chaos. It will not be just nation against nation, but "kingdom against kingdom"—indicating the political map of the world will need to be redrawn.

THE SIGNS OF HIS COMING

Where will it all end? Revelation 17 warns of the rise of a one-world religious system, which will unite all false religions just before the return of Christ to earth. Do you know the foundation for such a plan is already being laid? Powerful forces are at work today to create a united religions organization that mimics the United Nations in structure, scope, and authority.

The second sign Jesus predicted as a precursor of His return has to do with "wars and rumours of wars." In other words, the planet will be consumed in violence, revolution, upheaval, and chaos. It will not be just nation against nation, but "kingdom against kingdom"—indicating the political map of the world will need to be redrawn. Have we not seen the early stages of this phenomenon in the 1990s as one of the largest and most powerful empires of all time—the Soviet Union—imploded suddenly and almost without warning? Have we not witnessed the rise of another empire in the East as China emerges as an economic and military superpower? Have we not observed the maps of Eastern Europe and Central Asia being completely redrawn?

Today we see brother fighting against brother, tribe against tribe, in Albania, Rwanda, Bosnia, Kosovo, Sudan, and of course in the Middle East—the center stage for the unfolding prophetic drama. But there's more. Jesus continued, "And there shall be famines, and pestilences, and earthquakes, in diverse places" (Matthew 24:7). Famines? Recently I reported in the *Van Impe Intelligence Briefing* that the world's leading agricultural scientists say we are headed for an unprecedented global food shortage beyond the scope of anything modern man can imagine. They said that because the developing world's population is expected to grow by 2 billion in the next few years, those countries least able to produce food will need at least 75 percent more. Yet, despite advances in technology, food production around the world is growing at its slowest rate in four decades and is actually on the decline in at least ninety countries. Grain stocks are at their lowest levels in thirty-five years.

Global incidences of cholera, tuberculosis, diphtheria, and bubonic plague have skyrocketed in the past five years. The mosquito-borne illness dengue, which produces deadly fevers, has shown up in Latin America and the Caribbean for the first time in more than twenty years.

DISEASES THAT WON'T GO AWAY

Pestilences? It would have been hard to imagine, even a generation ago, that the world would be preoccupied with infectious diseases and plagues. After all, thanks to immunizations and better drugs, scientists confidently predicted the demise of many common, yet threatening, illnesses. Some even went on record to say that certain diseases would soon be gone forever. How wrong they were. Not only have these diseases refused to go away, they have increased dramatically. Not only in the under-developed nations, but here in North America as well. Even leaving deadly AIDS out of the equation, common infections such as pneumonia kill more people than ever. Why? Because of their growing resistance to the very antibiotics that were supposed to save us. As grave as the situation is in the United States, it is even worse through-out the rest of the world. Global incidences of cholera, tuberculosis, diphtheria, and bubonic plague have sky-rocketed in the past five years. The mosquito-borne ill-ness dengue, which produces deadly fevers, has shown up in Latin America and the Caribbean for the first time in more than twenty years. Another factor in the spread of disease is the new levels of international travel and mixing of populations that has occurred only in the lat-ter part of the twentieth century. As Nobel laureate Joshua Lederberg put it, "We have created the perfect world for the bugs to take over."

Earthquakes? Is it our imagination or have more and more violent quakes shaken the tectonic plates of our earth in recent years? Or is it simply that better technol-ogy allows us to measure them and report them to the world instantaneously? Perhaps it is both. The truth is we are witnessing a dramatic upsurge in earthquake and volcanic activity throughout the globe. According to the

U.S. Geological Survey, from 1890 to 1930, there were only eight quakes measuring 6.0 or larger. From 1930 to 1960, there were eighteen. From 1960 to 1979, however, there were sixty-four "killer" quakes. And from 1980 to 1996, there were more than two hundred. Plus, in concluding the present millennium, a devastating quake killing thousands and leaving tens of thousands homeless just occurred in Turkey.

What does Jesus tell us next? "Then shall they deliver you up to be afflicted, and shall kill you: and ye shall be hated of all nations for my name's sake" (Matthew 24:9). This worldwide persecution of the Church is taking place in increasing numbers and nations even as you read these words. Christians in North America are suddenly awakening to the extent of the slaughter and repression of believers in Communist and Islamic nations. I've just seen a report that indicates Christians in India and in many Muslim nations are being hunted down and persecuted in record numbers. Michael Horowitz of the Hudson Institute has called Christians "the Jews of the 21st century." The horrors are unspeakable in some Islamic countries, where Christians are being literally crucified for their faith. In China, the underground church—members of which are subject to arrest just for reading the Bible—is said to be larger than the entire evangelical community in the United States. Even here in the enlightened West, we are seeing the emergence of anti-Christian bigotry in the media, in government, and in the popular culture.

> Think about the divorce rate. Is not unfaithfulness or adultery the ultimate form of betrayal—whether it is at the highest level of government or in the bedroom of the average citizen?

THE STRUGGLE WILL CONTINUE

"And then shall many be offended, and shall betray one another, and shall hate one another," Jesus says in Matthew 24:10. Does this sound familiar? Have you ever known a time in history in which people are so easily offended over nothing? Now that the Ten Commandments have been relegated to the scrap heap by the world—and considered by many to be simply the *Ten Suggestions*—absolute standards of right and wrong are no longer in vogue. So now we have new sets of rules— wacky laws and regulations that cause a six-year-old boy to be kicked out of school for innocently kissing a girl on the cheek. "Sexual harassment," they called it. This in an age in which all too many schoolchildren carry guns to school and take drugs. Think about the divorce rate. Is not unfaithfulness or adultery the ultimate form of betrayal—whether it is at the highest level of government or in the bedroom of the average citizen? That's the world we're living in today—a world in which no one knows whom to trust anymore, a world in which nothing, not even the most loving relationships, seems permanent and lasting. A world that is leaping headlong toward a seven-year Tribulation hour that, praise God, will be followed by an era of peace such as the world has never known. However, we are not quite there yet!

So let's continue. Think about the enmity people have for one another around the world. It's not just nation rising up against nation; it's brother fighting with brother. Look at Bosnia and Rwanda where people who look like one another, and even speak the same language, are merciless in their blood lust and commitment to *ethnic cleansing*. The latest killing field is Albania, where civil war is wreaking havoc because the people feel "betrayed" by their own government.

Furthermore, in the last days, not only will people look to false Christs, but will also flock to false prophets (Matthew 24:5, 11, 24). Today, we see self-proclaimed gurus, many of whom wear clerical garb, telling us we are being misled by the truth of the Holy Scriptures. They suggest a *better way*, or multiple ways, or more convenient ways, or ways that do not offend the masses, reaching for heaven. They misrepresent the Word of God. They distort it. They read it out of context. They ignore passages they do not like. They search in vain for new passages to misinterpret that validate their blasphemous beliefs. In addition to quasi-Christians peddling a false gospel, we have the New Age charlatans spreading demonically inspired ideas about channeling, chanting, and other neopagan myths, relying on crystals instead of

Christ. Because of this situation, Jesus said, "The love of many shall wax cold" (Matthew 24:12).

But the news, even in this trying time, is not all bad. God is still in charge. One day He will bring ultimate peace to our world. However, that time has not yet come. Jesus said, "And this gospel of the kingdom shall be preached in all the world for a witness unto all nations" (verse 14). Then and only then, Jesus says, shall the end come, meaning the end of this age, not the world. Then Jesus, our Lord and Savior, shall appear with lightning speed in a blaze of glory (Matthew 24:27).

> And no signs are more important than the rebirth of the state of Israel in 1948 and the recapturing of Jerusalem by the Jews in 1967. The sheer existence of Israel is a testament to the truth of the prophets and the fact that God keeps His word.

Do you realize that only in this age of modern communications and world travel could even the most isolated peoples be reached with the Word of God? Today it is happening! The same technology that makes global government a threat makes it easier than ever to blanket the globe with the truth. That's what our ministry is all about: fulfilling the Great Commission. Did you know that more than 6,000 languages are spoken in this world today? Never before has the Bible been translated into so many of these tongues—even some spoken by obscure tribal peoples with no access to radio, television, or even the written word.

Yes, my friends, so much is happening in our world today to show that we are the generation about which Jesus spoke in Matthew 24:34. And no signs are more important than the rebirth of the state of Israel in 1948 and the recapturing of Jerusalem by the Jews in 1967. The sheer existence of Israel is a testament to the truth of the prophets and the fact that God keeps His word.

"And they shall fall by the edge of the sword, and shall be led away captive into all nations: and Jerusalem shall be trodden down of the Gentiles, until the times of the Gentiles be fulfilled. And there shall be signs in the sun, and in the moon, and in the stars; and upon the earth distress of nations, with perplexity; the sea and the waves roaring; Men's hearts failing them for fear, and for looking after those things which are coming on the earth: for the powers of heaven shall be shaken. And then shall they see the Son of man coming in a cloud with power and great glory. And when these things begin to come to pass, then look up, and lift up your heads; for your redemption draweth nigh." And he spake to them a parable; "Behold the fig tree, and all the trees; When they now shoot forth, ye see and know of your own selves that summer is now nigh at hand. So likewise ye, when ye see these things come to pass, know ye that the kingdom of God is nigh at hand.

Verily I say unto you, This generation shall not pass away, till all be fulfilled." (Luke 21:24-32)

JESUS IS COMING SOON

So the good news is that Jesus is returning! He is coming back! And this time, He's staying on earth to rule personally for a thousand years. Even that is only the beginning, because after that He continues to reign over an earthly kingdom forever—in a world without end. (Isaiah 9:7; Isaiah 45:17; Luke 1:33; Ephesians 3:21; and Hebrews 1:8.) The prayer of every believer should be "even so, come, Lord Jesus" (Revelation 22:20).

THE NATIONS ARE JUDGED

Now let's fast-forward the clock and return to the subject at hand. The terrible seven years of Tribulation have ended. Prophecy after prophecy has been fulfilled, and we have now entered the glorious Millennium, that thousand-year period of calm and serenity that has come about solely because Christ is our earthly Ruler and Lord. However, preceding this one-thousand-year reign, Jesus judges the nations. This occurs in the valley of Jehoshaphat, in the Kidron Valley, below the eastern gate following the battle of Armageddon. I have always thought it ironic that Christ will judge the nations in the same spot where He was betrayed—the garden of

Gethsemane. Now you may ask, Why will Jesus judge the nations? What have they done to deserve this judgment? First, a point of clarification: This is not the judgment of Revelation 20:11-15, that general judgment of the world, which we call the Great Judgment Day. The judgment to which we now refer is the one that prepares the people for the Millennial reign, the thousand-year rule of Christ upon earth. In Matthew 25:31-46, we see God judging the nations because the world's inhabitants did or did not receive Christ, did or did not receive the mark of the beast, and because they did or did not persecute Yahweh's wife, the Jews.

Let's delve deeper to establish who these people are. First, there are the ones—on the *right,* according to Scripture—who have shown love for the Jewish people and then for all people because of the Spirit of Christ living within them. These accepted the message of Christ's kingdom including their belief in the efficacy of the Cross and the shed blood of our Savior (John 1:29). And what does Christ say to those who have shown love and have prepared their hearts by receiving the message of Calvary? "Come, ye blessed of my Father, inherit the kingdom prepared for you from the foundation of the world" (Matthew 25:34). I cannot think of anything more exciting in Scripture than to realize that the coming of the King was planned from the creation and foundation of the world. Now all is ready, and He says to those who believe, "Come! Your hearts are ready. You have believed, and now you will receive your reward—that is to live with Me on earth for one thousand glorious years."

> Only those who have accepted Jesus as Savior and Lord will enter this new kingdom and enjoy the great and glorious beginning of the next phase of life. Satan has been bound, and the saved are entering the kingdom.

THE ULTIMATE PURGING

But what of the others, those on the "left hand" who demonstrated hatred toward so many? These are the bigots, the racists, those who thrived on the venom of anti-Semitism, who failed to come to the Cross to receive the Savior's forgiveness. These individuals sought neither a new heart nor a changed life through Christ's work at Calvary. What happens to those who missed the mark? Matthew 25:41 says, "Then shall he say also unto them on the left hand, Depart from me, ye cursed, into everlasting fire." That is the ultimate purging as the lost are eliminated. Only those who have accepted Jesus enter the earthly kingdom and enjoy the great and glorious beginning of the next phase of life. Satan has been bound, and the saved are entering and enjoying the kingdom for which believers prayed for centuries (Matthew 6:10). No sinners remain to influence the redeemed for evil. Something else is extremely interesting in this context. In

Daniel 12:11 and 12, we see a mention of 1,290 and 1,335 days. This passage says, "And from the time that the daily sacrifice shall be taken away, and the abomination that maketh desolate set up, there shall be a thousand two hundred and ninety days. Blessed is he that waiteth, and cometh to the thousand three hundred and five and thirty days." What is the significance of these numbers? Clearly, we know the Tribulation period will last 2,520 days because that is exactly seven years long (Daniel 9:27). A Jewish month was 30 days, so if you multiply 30 days a month by 12 months you get 360, and 7 years of that becomes 2,520, and one-half of that becomes 1,260. Note that in Revelation 11:3 and Revelation 12:6 it talks about the final 1,260-day reign of Antichrist. What does it mean? As mentioned previously, we know that the Tribulation period will last 2,520 days according to the Jewish calendar (Daniel 9:27). Now one-half of that is 1,260 days. But what about the 1,290 days? Why the additional 30 days? Because when Christ comes, the first thing He does is destroy the Antichrist, his works, and the false prophet by casting them into the lake of fire. We see this in Revelation 19:20, "And the beast was taken, and with him the false prophet that wrought miracles before him, with which he deceived them that had received the mark of the beast, and them that worshipped his image. These both were cast alive into a lake of fire burning with brimstone." So Christ judges the corruption that has existed under the regime of these evil ones and that takes

30 days. Next, the text mentions 45 additional days for a total of 1,335. Why? Because Christ judges the nations and their inhabitants. But how can He possibly do this in such a short period of time? Because believers who returned with Him share in the judgment of the world (1 Corinthians 6:2), and with their help this momentous event is accomplished in the extra forty-five-day period. And then what a time of rejoicing this will be as Christ ushers in a theocracy—the rule of God upon earth for centuries to come. Many continue to misunderstand that it is only *after* the thousand years when Christ is recommissioned that the eternal kingdom continues in total perfection. Please don't misunderstand. Righteous living will occur *during* the Millennium *but not a time of perfection,* because those who entered the kingdom after the judgment of the nations in Matthew 25 will still be housed in normal bodies containing old natures, which their children shall inherit. Because of this situation, millions rebel against Christ's authority through their descendants at the conclusion of the thousand years (Revelation 20:7-10).

It's important to remember that when we, the raptured, return with Christ to that Holy City of Revelation 21:9 to 22:15, we will have bodies that no longer sin because they will be like our Lord's. We were translated, changed, made new creations *on the way up* (Philippians 3:21). But those who remained still have their old bodies containing the old Adamic nature. They will still procreate and have children, and their children will have children who can sin. Because of this situation, Christ must rule the nations with a rod of iron (Psalm 2:9; Revelation 19:15).

> I've always felt if the Lord can't convince people of His power and majesty after a thousand years of earthly reign, that it's nothing short of amazing that when we preach the gospel in our day, people are *actually saved and begin their walk with the Lord.*

THE RULE OF THE ROD OF IRON

Because Christ establishes a theocracy on earth, He now administers His power to subdue mankind's stubborn natures (Psalm 2:9). But that's not all. He also rules with a rod of iron to keep people in line even when there's no devil to tempt them, even when there's no worldliness allowed, no riotous living, because of Christ's control over the subjects of His kingdom. Imagine. Millions go into His kingdom as righteous people but bear children who turn away from the Lord. I've always felt if the Lord can't convince people of His power and majesty after a thousand years of earthly reign, that it's nothing short of amazing that when we preach the gospel in our day, people are *actually saved and begin their walk with the Lord.* I have always seen this as one of the greatest miracles of all.

Other questions I am often asked is whether the devil is bound during this time, and if Jesus is on earth ruling and reigning with a rod of iron, how is it possible for sin to remain so rampant? Here is the answer. Three things make us sin: the world, the flesh, and the devil. First, the devil becomes helpless and is ruled out of the picture because Christ comes and binds Satan for a thousand years (Revelation 20:1-3) and casts him into the bottomless pit. Second, because Christ rules with a rod of iron, there will be no strip shows, no pornography, no drunkenness, no drug addiction, and no overt expression of evil of any kind. Christ simply will not allow it (Revelation 19:15). So what is left? The flesh! Remember there are still great multitudes in the Millennium with bodies possessing old natures and James 1:13-14 states: "Let no man say when he is tempted, I am tempted of God: for God cannot be tempted with evil, neither tempteth he any man: But every man is tempted, when he is drawn away of his own lust, and enticed." So sin occurs because of mankind's fleshly bodies and natures. Therefore, since "the wages of sin is death" (Romans 6:23), and "sin, when it is finished, bringeth forth death" (James 1:15), mankind must still die (Isaiah 65:20). This, however, will not include the raptured who already have glorified bodies and enjoy a sinless life in this Holy City hovering above the earth. They can never die again. Nevertheless, the good news concerning the earth dwellers is that sin is limited, making it possible for people to live extended and lengthy lives during the Millennium. In fact, Isaiah 65:20 says that a child, at one hundred years of age, is considered to be practically a teenager because sin, which brings death, is vastly limited under Christ's rule. So people will still be able to sin, but in a limited environment, and because of it live happier and longer lives. But let me say it again, the ones who hover above the earth in the Holy City, the ones who returned with Christ and are in their new glorified bodies, cannot sin. They live eternally in the Holy City, beginning with the thousand-year reign of Christ as well as during Christ's eternal kingdom upon earth after the Millennium. In this final kingdom on earth, all its inhabitants will have received glorified bodies and thus make sin impossible forever. Presently, the stage is set for this era of righteousness and peace. Soon we will have heaven on earth, forever fulfilling the prayer stated in Matthew 6:10, "Thy kingdom come. Thy will be done in earth, as it is in heaven."

"When the Son of man shall come in his glory,
and all the holy angels with him, then shall he sit upon
the throne of his glory."
(Matthew 25:31)

CHAPTER 6

A GOVERNMENT OF RIGHTEOUSNESS

I am often asked if there are terms or concepts in the Word of God that might be synonymous with the Millennium, the thousand-year reign of Christ when the earth is blanketed with universal peace and serenity. Throughout the Bible numerous terms describe this period of tranquillity to be administered under a righteous governance. Here are a few New Testament portions with their corresponding Millennium references in italics:

1. Matthew 5:10 says, "Blessed are they which are persecuted for righteousness' sake: for their's is the *kingdom of heaven.*"

2. In Matthew 19:28 we read, "And Jesus said unto them, 'Verily I say unto you, That ye which have followed me, in the *regeneration* when the Son of man shall sit in the throne of his glory, ye also

shall sit upon twelve thrones, judging the twelve tribes of Israel.'"

3. John 6:40 says, "And this is the will of him that sent me, that every one which seeth the Son, and believeth on him, may have everlasting life: and I will raise him up at the *last day.*"

4. Acts 3:19 makes a reference to the Millennium: "Repent ye therefore, and be converted, that your sins may be blotted out, when the *times of refreshing* shall come from the presence of the Lord."

5. Again in Acts we read, "Whom the heaven must receive until *the times of restitution of all things,* which God hath spoken by the mouth of all his holy prophets since the world began" (Acts 3:21).

6. And multiple verses in the Epistles refer to the Millennium. For instance, "Who shall also confirm you unto the end, that ye may be blameless *in the day of our Lord Jesus Christ*" (1 Corinthians 1:8; see also Philippians 4:5; 2 Thessalonians 2:7-10; Hebrews 9:28; 1 Peter 4:13; and Revelation 1:7).

After so many centuries of earth's travail with endless wars, sickness, animosity, and strife, finally and mercifully there will be *times of refreshing*.

A GREAT HARVEST OF SOULS

If you have never thought of the Millennium in this overarching biblical context, I want you to realize that the thousand-year reign of Christ is much more than simply ten centuries of divine rule. It is, in fact, the rule of Christ and His Bride who descended from heaven to complete the *regeneration* of our planet. After so many centuries of earth's travail wherein we have experienced endless wars, sickness, animosity, and strife, there will finally be *times of refreshing,* not the transitory *pause* that refreshes such as we have become accustomed to, but the kind of long-lasting, spiritual refreshment only God can provide for His people. And yes, ultimately there will be a *restitution of all things*—when all is made new, and when an original, pristine, Garden of Eden environment will again be the order of the day, because it will indeed be the *day of our Lord Jesus Christ.* And it will all take place under a government of righteousness and holiness such as the world has never experienced since Adam's fall.

> Christ's rule will be real. People will know, firsthand, God's enormous, divine power.

VARIOUS VIEWS OF THE KINGDOM

Before we move directly into our discussion of the *righteous government of the future kingdom,* I think it would be instructive to review a summary of the various positions that have been espoused regarding what this kingdom will actually look like. Rather than paraphrase the thinking of the great J. Dwight Pentecost, I want to quote him directly on this subject:

> To some the kingdom of God is synonymous with the eternal state, or heaven, into which one comes after death, so that it has no relationship to the earth whatsoever. To others it is a non-material or "spiritual" kingdom in which God rules over the hearts of men, so that, while it is related to the present age, it is unrelated to the earth. To still others the kingdom is purely earthly without spiritual realities attached to it, so that it is a political and social structure to be achieved by the efforts of men and thus becomes the goal of the social and economic evolution to which men press. To others with the same general concept, it has to do with a nationalistic movement on the part of Israel that will reconstitute that nation as an independent nation in the political realm. Then there are those who view the kingdom as synonymous with the visible organized church, so that the church becomes the kingdom, thus making the kingdom both spiritual and political. In addition there are those that view the kingdom as a manifestation, in the earthly realm, of the universal sovereignty of God, in which He rules in the affairs of men, so that the kingdom is conceived of being both

spiritual and material in its concept. Through this maze of interpretations it is almost impossible to make one's way. The truths related to the kingdom will not be derived by an examination of the writings of men, but rather only by an inductive study of the teaching of the Word of God on this great subject.[1]

To Pentecost's final sentence I can only say, *stop, look, and listen!* As we do, we cannot help but conclude that the Millennial government will be an earthly kingdom—a theocracy—the rule of God on earth, thereby distinguishing it from a strictly "spiritual reign" that may have occurred in the hearts of humankind through the many centuries of human history. Christ's rule will be real. People will know, firsthand, God's enormous, divine power.

But what will the Millennial government look like? First, Scripture counsels us to recognize the validity of *more than one* aspect of the kingdom. We have already stated our position that the Millennial form of Christ's earthly reign is not fulfilled exclusively by a "rule of God" in the hearts of men. This is not what the Bible teaches. His Millennial rule is literal, not figurative. This Millennial Kingdom must be regarded as the zenith of the prophetic program of God as it relates to the theocratic kingdom or Christ's rule of the earth. To some degree, this began in the creation of earth's first man, Adam, in the Garden of Eden, continued through eons of every conceivable form of human government, was demonstrated repeatedly in the kingly line that ruled Israel, and has its culmination in the Millennial Kingdom, which in turn is superseded by the timeless eternity that follows. I know that is a mouthful, but that has been the progression of events from the Garden of Eden to the present. Though there is, to some degree, a rule of God in the age in which you and I now live that could be described by the word *kingdom,* this rule does not yet fulfill those prophecies that speak directly to the Millennial reign of Christ upon the earth. However, as good as earth will *become* at the close of Christ's thousand-year reign, it will be in no manageable shape upon His Second Advent.

> Medical authorities of the world said recently that almost thirty-three million people on earth are infected with HIV, two-thirds of them in sub-Saharan Africa.

EARTH WILL BE A MESS

Because the earth will be in such economic, political, and environmental shambles when the Lord returns, it will take every bit of Christ's rule of iron to make things happen. We cannot be specific about how earth will look during that period, but we can surmise the degree of degradation and decomposition by what we see on earth now. Let me give you just three examples of where we are today. I'll simply ask you to let your imagination soar as you think of how planet earth might look during the early years of the Millennium. Today, despite worldwide education and awareness programs, the medical authorities of the world said recently that almost thirty-three million people on earth are infected with HIV, two-thirds of them in sub-Saharan Africa. A World Health Organization report estimated there would be two million AIDS deaths in the region by the end of this year. It said that almost six million more people would be infected this year with the HIV virus that causes AIDS. The Associated Press has reported that according to the UN's top AIDS official, Dr. Peter Piot, an increasing AIDS crisis has "crept up on South Africa." He was quoted as saying, "We are faced with an unprecedented crisis," which he said is worse than apartheid, South Africa's former system of white minority rule.

If that is not enough bad news, Reuters reports new research that indicates one out of every 1,000 Americans could be walking around infected with HIV without even knowing it. A new study in "low-risk" people revealed this disturbing news in light of a new urine test that has detected the AIDS virus in people *who showed no signs of infection in their blood*. Researchers said that this now could explain why people mysteriously die of AIDS without having signs of HIV infection. They also said this fact could possibly help determine why some people resist infection (Revelation 6:7-8).

However, the spread of AIDS is not the only plague on all our houses. The BBC recently reported that because of

Russia's overcrowded prison system, another deadly disease is on the march. The report noted that prisoners have a new untreatable form of tuberculosis (TB) that is spreading with terrifying speed. Ten percent of Russia's one million prisoners suffer from TB and 20 percent of them are thought to have the drug-resistant strain—which means 20,000 face certain death. The disease multiplies in the festering conditions of Russia's overcrowded cells. In many prisons inmates have to sleep in shifts. Poor diet, stress, and depressed immune systems make the prisoners vulnerable targets. Prison clinics cannot afford to treat patients with the full course of drugs, so the disease becomes resistant and even more difficult and expensive to cure. *Russia's penal system is becoming a time bomb for the rest of the world.* Once TB-infected prisoners step outside the prison gates, there is nothing to stop them from spreading the disease onto the streets of Russian cities and beyond. Most of the people standing outside a European charity-run clinic in Moscow are ex-prisoners. Many of them have TB and all are homeless. Because they are not registered with the city authorities, the Russian health system refuses to treat them.

> "For nation shall rise against nation, and kingdom against kingdom: and there shall be famines, and pestilences, and earthquakes, in divers places. All these are the beginning of sorrows" (Matthew 24:7-8).

Reuters has also reported that the former Soviet republic of Kazakhstan faces a tuberculosis epidemic similar to that in Russia if urgent measures to stem its spread are not taken immediately. A health official was quoted as saying that practically *every person in the country has failed to receive any defense against this disease.* No one is immune, and new cases of tuberculosis are occurring all the time. We have to take urgent measures. The report went on to say that cases of the highly contagious disease rose by 17,000 in the first eleven months of 1998 to reach 73,000, out of a total population of about 16 million. My friend, here is what God's Word has to say about where we are and where we are heading: "For nation shall rise against nation, and kingdom against kingdom: and there shall be famines, and pestilences, and earthquakes, in divers places. All these are the beginning of sorrows" (Matthew 24:7-8).

These predictions are coming true: Hong Kong's *South China Morning Post* recently went on record to report that North Korea is in a state of war readiness and is holding mass rallies to whip up anti-American hatred. Commanders of combat troops have been sent to the demilitarized zone separating the two Koreas, while the general staff is drawing up a comprehensive plan to repel an expected invasion by American-led forces. The North Koreans anticipate air strikes against an underground facility the United States suspects is nuclear-related, with an all-out war to follow. North Koreans believe the

Americans have drawn up an invasion plan, code-named "5027," and that an attack may be imminent. All this in the context of a communist nation that cannot feed itself and that is not able to refute reports of widespread cannibalism in the country.

The evidence is overwhelming that humankind has failed miserably as a steward of this planet. One of Russia's largest bodies of fresh water has already become a dead sea. The daily burning of huge areas of the Amazon rain forest destroys the lungs of the planet that produces the oxygen we cannot live without. Increasingly poor weather and erosion rapidly expand deserts of the Sahara, devastating northern Africa. *Deforestation* is the technical word; to the people who live there, the word is *hopelessness*. Our world and its people have suffered for thousands of years because of the curse of selfishness and sin. Today, whose lungs do not feel the effects of a debilitating smog from automobiles and industrial pollution that has killed millions and rendered others to a life of pain? Yes, it is bad now. But imagine, if you will, the ravages of the wars that will occur during the Great Tribulation and how they will further devastate our planet's delicate ecological systems. It will make the burning oil fields of Kuwait during the Gulf War look like a traditional Fourth of July barbecue. Praise God that Christ heals the planet's wounds when He establishes His Millennial Kingdom. However, and I will continually bring this to your attention, *while there will be a massive rebuilding program, it will not be presto chango, poof—all is now well!* It will not be that easy, and it will take years of harsh, righteous, dictatorial rule to set things straight.

> The first thing Christ will do will be to sit on His throne, where He will judge the nations for the express purpose of determining their status in the new kingdom.

THE STRATEGY AND THE TACTICS

So how will Christ revive, revitalize, and restore the earth? What will be His divine strategy, and what will He use to return earth to its original status? The greatest restoration program in history is called "the times of refreshing" (Acts 3:19), "the time of restitution" (Acts 3:21), and "the regeneration" (Matthew 19:28). The fulfillment of these verses may take years to complete; however, there is another occurrence that will take only days and is virtually necessary to have a kingdom of peace and righteousness. Let's consider this event. It begins as Christ judges the nations for the express purpose of determining their status as to whether they are fit subjects for the kingdom. The scenario is described in Matthew 25:31-34, 41:

> "When the Son of man shall come in his glory, and all
> the holy angels with him, then shall he sit upon the

throne of his glory: And before him shall be gathered all nations; and he shall separate them one from another, as a shepherd divideth his sheep from the goats: And he shall set the sheep on his right hand, but the goats on the left. Then shall the King say unto them on his right hand, Come, ye blessed of my Father, inherit the kingdom prepared for you from the foundation of the world: . . . Then shall he say also unto them on the left hand, Depart from me, ye cursed, into everlasting fire, prepared for the devil and his angels."

There is no doubt that the righteous rule of Christ will be administered with integrity and justice. However, because of mankind's hardness of heart, He will have to break stubborn wills among the redeemed with a rod of iron (Psalm 2:9; Revelation 19:15). Believe me, He won't be a wimp when He rules as the King of kings. Multitudes of leaders will be under His governance— under His thumb—whether they like it or not. These leaders may think they control their nation's affairs, running their traditional, status quo programs, when, in reality, they will be servants *doing our Lord's bidding*. Note these prophetic words from the pen of Zechariah, "The LORD shall be king over all the earth: in that day shall there be one LORD, and his name one" (14:9). And what will be the result of this religious/political authority that Jesus Christ commands over the earth? Two words: *righteousness* and *peace*. Isaiah 2:1-5 tells us,

The word that Isaiah the son of Amoz saw concerning Judah and Jerusalem. And it shall come to pass in the last days, that the mountain of the LORD's house shall be established in the top of the mountains, and shall be exalted above the hills; and all nations shall flow unto it. And many people shall go and say, Come ye, and let us go up to the mountain of the LORD, to the house of the God of Jacob; and he will teach us of his ways, and we will walk in his paths: for out of Zion shall go forth the law, and the word of the LORD from Jerusalem. And he shall judge among the nations, and shall rebuke many people: and they shall beat their swords into plowshares, and their spears into pruninghooks: nation shall not lift up sword against nation, neither shall they learn war any more. O house of Jacob, come ye, and let us walk in the light of the LORD.

All armaments will be scrapped. Finally, the promise of the great spiritual *I ain't gonna study war no more* will become a reality. The mere physical presence of our great God and Saviour Jesus Christ, ruling and reigning, will bring universal peace to earth. For centuries, men and women have promised peace to humankind. Politicians have guaranteed a "chicken in every pot." Every conceivable system of government has come and gone—all promising some degree of utopia. "The next election will make all things right," one promises. "Vote for me. I am the one who can turn the tables right side up. Put me in office and things will be different," says another. How foolish for us ever to believe a word of their hollow promises. It simply never happens. It will take the return of Christ to this earth to deal with the challenges of the insane and dangerous international situation in which the world finds itself today. What is the answer? Christ's Millennial Kingdom. How will Christ rule? Righteously, honestly, and lovingly, but as I already said, with a rod of iron. Nothing else will accomplish God's goals.

FROM HOLLOW SLOGANS TO GOD'S PROMISES

Today, with nations continuing to arm themselves to the hilt, the only way to meet this world's crisis is for our Lord to intervene in the physical affairs of man and set things straight. With false doctrines spreading through ecclesiastical circles like wildfire, shallow, uninformed New Age thinking on the increase, and blasphemy against the name of Jesus as commonplace as breathing, only the personal presence of the King can set things right. When this blessed time comes, Israel will be saved and living in her own unhindered land (Romans 11:26), while Satan will have been sent for one thousand years to writhe in the bottomless pit (Revelation 20:3). During the next thousand years, God will rule not only the nations, but the hearts of mankind as well. Zechariah 14:16 describes this glorious time: "And it shall come to pass, that every one that is left of all the nations which came against Jerusalem shall even go up from year to year to worship the King . . ."

However, there is one other matter to consider. Zechariah indicates that multitudes of unsaved people will also come into existence as they are born to the righteous believers who will have entered the kingdom at Christ's invitation (Matthew 25:34). Because they will be born with the old nature, multitudes of unsaved people will replenish the earth right down to the Millennium's final hour. Zechariah speaks of people from the Gentile nations who must appear in Jerusalem once a year to worship the King and to keep the Feast of Tabernacles. For those who fail to comply, there will be punishment (Zechariah 14:16-19). One would think that the theocracy (God's government upon earth) would see all humanity enamored and totally dedicated to Christ. Not so! That's why the children born to believers during the thousand years will reject Jesus and rebel against His reign at the conclusion of the one thousand years and after being in His presence for thirty to forty generations. Revelation 20:7-9 depicts God's judgment upon earth's final revolutionaries. Sad, isn't it? But let's move ahead and dwell rather upon the great things that happen during this Millennium.

There will be nonstop, universal peace for one thousand years. Law and order will prevail. Righteousness shall cover the earth. Pollution will be no more. Wheelchairs, walkers, and canes will be thrown aside. Isaiah 35:5-6 promises, "Then the eyes of the blind shall be opened, and the ears of the deaf shall be unstopped. Then shall the lame man leap as an hart, and the tongue of the dumb sing . . ." Living conditions will be ideal for health and comfort (Revelation 22:2). The universal curse placed by God upon the vegetable kingdom because of Adam's sin will have been removed. Farmland once useless will be fertile and productive. Isaiah says, "The wilderness and the solitary place shall be glad for them; and the desert shall rejoice, and blossom as the rose. It shall blossom abundantly, and rejoice even with joy and singing" (35:1-2). Amos echoes the words of Isaiah, "Behold, the days come, saith the LORD, that the plowman shall overtake the reaper, and the treader of grapes him that soweth seed; and the mountains shall drop sweet wine, and all the hills shall melt" (9:13). Can you imagine what life in the Millennium will be like? The trees that grow near the New River will receive their source of life from beneath the threshold of the throne of God, fed by life-giving waters (Revelation 22:1). Imagine! The leaves of these trees will not wither—they will produce a new crop of twelve different fruits each month and will be used for medicinal purposes (Revelation 22:2).

But there's even more. The universal curse will be removed from among the "survival of the fittest" animal kingdom so that the wolf also shall dwell with the lamb, and the leopard shall lie down with the kid; and the calf and the young lion and the fatling together; and a little child shall lead them. And the cow and the bear shall feed; their young ones shall lie down together: and the lion shall eat straw like the ox. And the suckling child shall play on the hole of the asp, and the weaned child shall put his hand on the cockatrice' den. They shall not hurt nor destroy in all my holy mountain (Isaiah 11:6-9).

There will even be a shift in the operation of the celestial bodies, possibly even a dramatic shifting of the poles of the earth, resulting in a universal climate that will eliminate the extremes of cold and heat we experience today (Isaiah 30:26). The physical health of humankind will so improve that today's "fitness craze" will go the way of unused treadmills and exercise bikes. If a person dies at the age of one hundred, *his neighbors will shake their heads in despair, lamenting that their friend died in mere infancy* (Isaiah 65:20). Such will be the golden age of the earth to be ushered in at the Second Advent of the Lord of Glory and governed righteously by our precious Lord Jesus.

Every valley shall be exalted, and every mountain and hill shall be made low: and the crooked shall be made straight, and the rough places plain: And the glory of the LORD shall be revealed, and all flesh shall see it together: for the mouth of the LORD hath spoken it.
(Isaiah 40:4-5)

CHAPTER 7

THE SPIRITUAL ENVIRONMENT OF THE MILLENNIUM

Have you ever noticed that when our Lord was on earth, He gave three cheers to those who needed encouragement most? First, in Matthew 9:2, He said to the man sick of the palsy, "Son, *be of good cheer;* thy sins be forgiven thee." This is the good cheer of pardon, and the starting point of all Christian life and experience, for without this declaration of divine forgiveness there can be no eternal relationship with the Father. The apostle Paul declared in Acts 13:38-39, "Be it known unto you . . . that through this man [Jesus] is preached unto you the forgiveness of sins: and by him all that believe are justified from all things." What good news! Then, in Matthew 14:22-27 we read the familiar story of what happened when Jesus dispatched His disciples to the other side of the lake while He made His way to a mountaintop to pray and spend time with His

Father. Picture the scene . . . in the middle of the sea, the boat began to encounter heavy winds. However, during the storm the Savior, now walking on the surface of the water, returned to his beleaguered group of followers, saying to them, "BE OF GOOD CHEER; it is I; be not afraid." This is the good cheer of comfort. He held their hands and calmed their frightened spirits. They were frantic, worried about whether they would live or die. However, while they were being tossed about by their fears, Jesus came to them in His perfect love and grace, bringing calm and quiet to their fainting hearts. Finally, in John 16:33 Jesus exclaimed, "In the world ye shall have tribulation: but BE OF GOOD CHEER; I have overcome the world." This is the good cheer of victory— an announcement that gives us hope in the midst of fear and confidence in times of trouble. The battle has been won. Victory is not in question. What a wonderful formula for enduring hope.

> People who are alive at the close of the Millennium will finally know the ultimate peace and comfort of Christ when He comes to rule and reign for one thousand glorious years.

ONE DAY SOON

Why do I start this chapter on the *spiritual life in the Millennium* with these words of cheer from the lips of

Jesus? For a simple reason: Our world desperately seeks peace of mind and quietness of heart and will try anything to get it—not much different, really, from the attitude of Christ's disciples. The main difference being that we are more likely to live out our frustrations and fears in offices, kitchens, crowded freeways, and family rooms than in small boats. However, in this quest for peace and contentment, we often overlook the obvious: a deep, personal relationship with the person of Jesus Christ that will *cheer us on* to victory. The good news, my friend, is that one day all this will change. And why? Because those who are alive at the close of the present millennium will ultimately know the peace and comfort of Christ when He comes to rule and reign for one thousand glorious years.

However, with the abundance of information and biblical evidence available today, the average Christian continues to misunderstand many facets of the Millennial period. Many believe that when Christ returns as King, all of creation will be fresh, new, and redeemed. The Bible says *not so*. Though the thousand years will be wonderful, it will still not be a time of total perfection because human beings will continue to possess the old Adamic nature, which will be passed down to their offspring. Only *after* the thousand years when all humanity receives glorified bodies will there be perfection. Let me explain the situation clearly. At the beginning of the Millennium, the world is in chaos, a condition already referred to in chapter 6. That is why in Matthew 19:28 we read that Christ's first act of business will be to regenerate the earth and breathe new life into a sorry situation. Acts 3:19 calls this period *the times of refreshing;* Acts 3:21, *the times of restitution.*

> **It may take forty or fifty years before a complete restitution or restoration takes place.**

THE REBUILDING WILL TAKE TIME

As you may remember from your reading of history—or perhaps from personal experience—it took many years to rebuild the nations of Europe after the devastation of World War II. The fierce, bloody battles were then history. The dead had been counted, and the wounded returned to their homes for rehabilitation and healing. The allies had clearly beaten the madman Hitler at his own sinister game. However, in the aftermath of war, there was still much to do. There was victory and peace, but the cure was almost as devastating as the pain. In the same way, it will take years to repair the massive damage that humankind does to planet earth during the Tribulation period. Christ *will,* however, do the job, and His modus operandi will be that of the spirit. This is why we must now attempt to understand the nature of the *spiritual environment* of the Millennium—the subject of this chapter.

To reiterate, before there can be global peace, there will be hard-fought battles and skirmishes for the hearts and minds of earth's people. This becomes clear as we read Revelation 6:3-8. The rider on the red horse will take peace from the earth, and suddenly there will be war on an unprecedented scale. Then the rider on the black horse will appear and create a season of worldwide famine. The rider on the pale horse will then gallop across earth's landscape at breakneck speed, spreading pestilence. These are ominous horses indeed. Then in Revelation 8:7, a third part of the trees will be burned as war plagues the planet. In Revelation 9:18 we read, "By these three was the third part of men killed, by the fire, and by the smoke, and by the brimstone." Revelation 16:3 reminds us that every living soul or creature will die in the sea because of pollution. Revelation 16:18 says, "There was a great earthquake, such as was not since men were upon the earth, so mighty an earthquake, and so great" . . . on and on it goes. I hope I have made it clear through repetition that this old world will be in a mess when Jesus returns. It will be in shambles, piles upon piles of rubble. It may take forty or fifty years before a complete restitution or restoration takes place. However, when Christ returns, the situation begins to change slowly and steadily but surely. But how will He accomplish His mission? What qualities will our Lord present to an unrepentant populace that will turn things around? What will spiritual life be like in the Millennium?

The lost tribes of Israel along with all other Jews who have not returned will hear this blaring "trumpet."

THE SALVATION OF ALL ISRAEL

First things first . . . *the salvation of the Jews.* In the epistle to the Romans, Paul writes: "God hath not cast away his people which he foreknew . . . For I would not, brethren, that ye should be ignorant of this mystery, lest ye should be wise in your own conceits; that blindness in part is happened to Israel, until the fulness of the Gentiles be come in. And so all Israel shall be saved: as it is written, There shall come out of Sion the Deliverer, and shall turn away ungodliness from Jacob: For this is my covenant unto them, when I shall take away their sins" (Romans 11:2a, 25-27). What is the significance of these verses? Simply this: The people and nation that crucified their Messiah at Christ's first advent will now be saved by the sovereign grace of God at His Second Coming. The prophet Zechariah speaks eloquently about this event stating: "I will pour upon the house of David, and upon the inhabitants of Jerusalem, the spirit of grace and of supplications: and they shall look upon me whom they have pierced, and they shall mourn for him [God the Son], as one who mourneth for his only son, and shall be in bitterness for him, as one that is in bitterness for his firstborn"

(Zechariah 12:10). Israel will slowly find herself both convinced and convicted of the sin of rejecting her Messiah and will mourn in repentance. Zechariah 13:1 says, "In that day there shall be a fountain opened to the house of David and to the inhabitants of Jerusalem for sin and for uncleanness." Israel's admission of sin will give special meaning to the words of the great hymn of the church: "There is a fountain filled with blood, drawn from Immanuel's veins, and sinners plunged beneath that flood, lose all their guilty stains." All Israel shall be saved, those who make the Middle East their home, including the lost tribes of Israel. Here's what our Lord says about this in connection with His Second Advent: "He shall send his angels with a great sound of a trumpet, and they shall gather together his elect from the four winds, from one end of heaven to the other" (Matthew 24:31). The lost tribes of Israel along with all other Jews who have not returned will hear this blaring "trumpet." Isaiah paints a graphic picture of how the lost tribes will identify themselves. He writes, "Fear not, O Jacob, my servant; and thou, Jesurun, whom I have chosen. For I will pour water upon him that is thirsty, and floods upon the dry ground: I will pour my spirit upon thy seed, and my blessing upon thine offspring: And they shall spring up as among the grass, as willows by the water courses. One shall say, I am the LORD's; and another shall call himself by the name of Jacob; and another shall subscribe with his hand unto the LORD, and surname himself by the name of Israel" (Isaiah 44:2-5). Could anything be plainer? The lost tribes will identify themselves as Jews through the pervasive ministry of the Holy Spirit of God. Therefore, after thousands of years of history, we finally begin to see the unraveling of the divine plot: Israel will be saved, and she will be saved in the context of a moral and spiritual kingdom.

> This kingdom of the here-and-now must not be equated with the *spiritual nature* of the Millennial Kingdom still to come.

THE HERE-AND-NOW VERSUS THE THERE-AND-THEN

Let me ask you a question: Do you believe there is a present spiritual kingdom, a rule of almighty God that exists in the hearts of humankind who are obedient, humble servants of the living God? I am sure your answer is probably yes! However, herein lies the confusion for many: This kingdom of the here-and-now must not be equated with the *spiritual nature* of the Millennial Kingdom still to come. For this reason: Spiritual life in the Millennium will be like nothing ever before seen in the history of the world. The primary—and most distinctive—feature will be a rule of Christ on earth devoid of even the remotest idea of a *materialistic concept* of the kingdom. We read in God's Word that the Millennium will be a reflection of those attributes of Christ that promise the highest standards of true spirituality. Given the earthly mess that must be corrected, nothing other than the highest order of spiritual leadership by Christ will be enough to accomplish the task.

THE PHYSICAL PRESENCE OF CHRIST: THE CRITICAL DIFFERENCE

Although throughout the centuries we have seen great revivals, culture-shaking reformations, massive rededications of people's hearts, and great periods of spiritual enlightenment, these will all pale when compared to the spiritual life of the Millennial Kingdom, and *for one key reason:* Christ in His power and majesty will be physically present during this all-new period of time. Do you remember Peter's prophecy? He writes in 1 Peter 1:10-11, "Of which salvation the prophets have enquired and searched diligently, who prophesied of the grace that should come unto you: Searching what, or what manner of time the Spirit of Christ which was in them did signify, when it testified beforehand the sufferings of Christ, and the glory that should follow." This glory becomes visible to all at Christ's Second Advent— described in Matthew 24:30, "And then shall appear the sign of the Son of man in heaven: and then shall all the tribes of the earth mourn, and they shall see the Son of man coming in the clouds of heaven with power and great glory."

Several other key passages of Scripture promise that the glory of Christ will be front and center on earth during the Millennium. Isaiah 40:4-5 tells us, "Every valley shall be exalted, and every mountain and hill shall be made low: and the crooked shall be made straight, and the rough places plain: And the glory of the LORD shall be revealed, and all flesh shall see it together: for the mouth of the LORD hath spoken it." Did you catch those eight words, "the glory of the LORD shall be revealed?" This is the message we have been singing so robustly in Handel's *Messiah* over the years. But no longer will these stirring words simply be a "song of the season." During the Millennium, they will be the song of the day. It will be number one on the charts! However, not only Isaiah predicts the nature of the spiritual kingdom during the Millennium. The psalmist also mentions it in Psalm 72:19, "Blessed be his glorious name for ever: and let the whole earth be filled with his glory; Amen, and Amen." The awesome, inexorable, all-prevailing glory of the God of Israel will be manifested in the person of Christ in superabundance. Hebrews 2:8 reminds us that those living during the Millennium will see Christ's majesty displayed in His *glorious dominion,* "Thou hast put all things in subjection under his feet. For in that he put all in subjection under him, he left nothing that is not put under him." Christ's power will also be seen in the *glorious inheritance of a Promised Land* (Daniel 8:9; 11:16, 41).

> Millennial people will see Christ's righteousness, His divine mercy, His manifest goodness, His unbridled holiness, His divine compassion, and His unfailing truth.

THE ATTRIBUTES OF GOD

As Christians, we know and revere the omnipotence, omniscience, and omnipresence of our holy God. These have always been at the center of our Christian belief. However, during the Millennial Kingdom these attributes of God as expressed in the person of Christ will be present for *all* to see. The world at large will know who is in command of events. Millennial people will see Christ's righteousness, His divine mercy, His manifest goodness, His unbridled holiness, His divine compassion, and His unfailing truth. Christ will be the center of worship and the focus of all spirituality. Throughout our years on this earth, you and I have done our part, hopefully, to announce the good news of Jesus Christ in our places of work, in our homes, in the media, and in our churches. Many who have heard the message of the gospel have had ears to hear *and they have accepted the claims of the Savior*. However, many have ignored the promises of God, choosing to go their own way. During the Millennium, however, it will be a different scene. It will be a season—a very long, thousand-year season—when the entire earth will, in the words of Isaiah 11:9, "be full of the knowledge of the LORD, as the waters cover the sea." Jeremiah 31:33-34 is even more descriptive, saying:

> This shall be the covenant that I will make with the house of Israel; After those days, saith the LORD, I will put my law in their inward parts, and write it in their hearts; and will be their God, and they shall be my people. And they shall teach no more every man his neighbour, and every man his brother, saying, Know the LORD: for they shall all know me, from the least of them unto the greatest of them, saith the LORD: for I will forgive their iniquity, and I will remember their sin no more.

> To have Christ write His personal love letter in one's heart is almost more than I can fathom.

A TIME OF JOY . . . A TIME OF PEACE

I don't know about you, but I literally get goose bumps when I read these two verses from Jeremiah. Think of it! The law will be put *in their inward parts.* It will be part of people's physical and spiritual makeup. Christ's message will be *written in their hearts.* Indelible ink may be one thing, but to have Christ write His personal love letter in one's heart is almost more than I can fathom. And this awesome thought— "And they shall teach no more every man his neighbour, and every man his brother, saying, Know the LORD: for they shall all know me." Imagine. The Word of God—and the person of Jesus Christ—will be so pervasive, such daily, front-page copy, that everyone will know the Lord! This, my friend, is the nature and spiritual environment of the Millennium.

It will be a period of righteousness as Psalm 72:7 predicts: "In his days shall the righteous flourish." The prophet Isaiah puts even more teeth into the nature of this righteousness stating: "But with righteousness shall he judge the poor, and reprove with equity for the meek of the earth: and he shall smite the earth with the rod of his mouth, and with the breath of his lips shall he slay the wicked. And righteousness shall be the girdle of his loins, and faithfulness the girdle of his reins" (Isaiah 11:4-5).

But it is not righteousness simply for the sake of righteousness, but rather the prelude to universal peace as predicted in Micah 4:3 and Isaiah 2:4, which says, "He shall judge among the nations, and shall rebuke many people: and they shall beat their swords into plowshares, and their spears into pruninghooks: nation shall not lift up sword against nation, neither shall they learn war any more." That, my friend, is what peace will be like. Finally, the desire of the ages for peace will be the order of the day.

It will lead to a time of joy unimaginable. In fact, this spirit of joy will be the hallmark of Christ's thousand-year reign. In your mind's eye, I want you to see Isaiah wiping tears of happiness from his eyes as he writes,

> Behold, God is my salvation; I will trust, and not be afraid: for the LORD JEHOVAH is my strength and my song; he also is become my salvation. Therefore with joy shall ye draw water out of the wells of salvation. And in that day shall ye say, Praise the LORD, call upon his name, declare his doings among the people, make mention that his name is exalted. Sing unto the LORD; for he hath done excellent things: this is known in all the earth. Cry out and shout, thou inhabitant of Zion: for great is the Holy One of Israel in the midst of thee. (Isaiah 12:2-6)

What a grand turnabout it will be! There will be garlands for ashes, cruses of the oil of joy for those who mourn, beautiful garments of praise for those afflicted with a spirit of heaviness; instead of shame, we read, "ye shall have double." Imagine the generosity of our wonderful Christ: those who have land will find it doubled, even as everlasting joy is made available to all, landholders or not! (Isaiah 61:3, 7).

> Spirituality during the Millennium will be based on the truth of God as manifested through Him who rules with a rod of iron, Jesus Christ.

THE TEMPLE AND THE WORSHIP
OF THE ONE TRUE GOD

Ultimately, in the spiritual kingdom of the Millennium there will be no New Age charlatans. There will be no more spiritual fraud, bad theology, or half-baked interpretation of Scripture. Spirituality during the Millennium will be based on the truth of God as manifested through Him who rules with a rod of iron, Jesus Christ. Now, I want to share some insights that I am sure will pique your interest and will provide you with an even deeper understanding into how people of the Millennium will experience the "temple" aspects of Christ's reign. First, we need to remember that, presently, the Jews are preparing to build a third temple in Jerusalem for worship. What some do not realize is that *this becomes the temple where the Antichrist sits.* It cannot be the fourth temple of Ezekiel 40–48 that Jesus occupies. This third temple—not the fourth, but the third—will be defiled by the great traitor and impostor. In this third temple where *Antichrist* sits, we know there will be sacrifices because Daniel 9:27 says he, in his fury, terminates all sacrifices after forty-two months of his reign. Some are puzzled as to why sacrifices are necessary. Was not the work of Christ sufficient when He died at Calvary, *crying, "It is finished"?* Yes, a million times yes. However, Jewish sacrifices will occur for the same reason that Christians remember Christ's sacrifice today. It is called *commun-*

ion, and we read of its significance in 1 Corinthians 11:23-26:

> For I have received of the Lord that which also I delivered unto you, That the Lord Jesus the same night in which he was betrayed took bread: And when he had given thanks, he brake it, and said, "Take, eat: this is my body, which is broken for you: this do in remembrance of me." After the same manner also he took the cup, when he had supped, saying, "This cup is the new testament in my blood: this do ye, as oft as ye drink it, in remembrance of me." For as often as ye eat this bread, and drink this cup, ye do shew the Lord's death till he come.

At His return, our present memorial service will be passé. During the Millennium, however, because the Jews are under another dispensation, they will offer sacrifices, not because the work of Christ was insufficient, but rather as a memorial service to the Lamb of God who died for them. They will, in essence, be saying, *"We now bring our loving remembrance to You because of what You did for us on the cross to provide for our remission of sins."* This is why the Antichrist, in bias, hatred, and fury, stops the memorial service after a period of forty-two months and desecrates the holy temple through his false prophet by building an image in his likeness and *placing it in the temple* (Revelation 13:15). This becomes a flagrant violation of the commandment of the Jews in Exodus 20 that says, "Thou shalt not make unto thee any graven image." Daniel says it would become "the abomination that maketh desolate," or more clearly, the abomination of an image that makes the holy temple desolate and unholy (Daniel 11:31 and 12:11).

Keep in mind, however, that while all this God-dishonoring business is going on, an underlying movement of peace and prosperity waits in the wings. Soon everything will change as Messiah breaks through the blue to set up His glorious kingdom. Then war will be utterly unknown. Not a single armament plant will be operating; not a soldier or sailor will be in uniform. No military camps will exist, and not one cent will be spent for weapons of destruction. Can you imagine such an age, when all nations experience perfect peace? Can you imagine an age when there will be no poverty, when everyone will have all his or her needs supplied, and when violence and crime will be practically unknown as Christ subdues humanity (Psalm 2:9)? Can you imagine a time when there will be no wastelands, no storms, no droughts, no crop failures, no floods, when even the wild animals will be tame and harmless and will cease devouring one another (Isaiah 11:6-9)? If you ask me where you can find such information, you simply need to turn to your Bible, to the living Word of God, for it is replete with that glorious coming age of full redemption and creation's restoration.

I want to close this chapter with a paragraph from the great student of prophecy J. Dwight Pentecost, who writes,

> By the establishment of the theocracy on earth for a thousand years, under the Messianic theocratic King, God has accomplished His purpose of demonstrating His rule in the sphere in which that authority was first challenged. By merging this earthy theocracy with the eternal kingdom God's eternal sovereignty is established. Such was the purpose of God in planning the theocratic kingdom and developing it through successive stages through history until it reaches the climax of the program in the theocracy under the enthroned Christ in the millennium. That authority, which Satan first challenged, Christ has now demonstrated belongs solely to God. God's right to rule is eternally vindicated.[1]

The great Millennium is coming . . . and it will be a thousand years as no other.

And the cow and the bear shall feed; their young ones
shall lie down together: and the lion
shall eat straw like the ox.
And the sucking child shall play on the hole of the asp,
and the weaned child shall put his hand
on the cockatrice' den.
They shall not hurt nor destroy in all my holy mountain: for the earth shall be full of the knowledge of the
LORD, as the waters cover the sea.
(Isaiah 11:7-9)

CHAPTER 8

LIFE IN
THE MILLENNIUM

A *View from Above*

I will say it again. The subject of the Millennium remains one of the most misunderstood concepts among Christians today. Many present-day believers are thoroughly confused about this biblically vital thousand-year period. For instance, many believe that Russia must march at the inception of the seven-year Tribulation period and be defeated within the first few weeks of the conflict. This, in their minds, is imperative so that the burning of weapons for seven years (Ezekiel 39:9) will be completed before a perfect world under the Messiah can be established. However, in studying the scholarship of more than 130 authors, I have concluded that the teaching of the thousand-year reign of Christ has often been mythicized and erroneously taught from many of our nation's pulpits and Bible seminars. I also believe I know why such confusion reigns.

The signs are all around us. Because of humankind's unbridled avarice and the destructive results of polluting its own nest, the earth's ecosystems are fast breaking down. Worse yet, as people continue to turn away from God and His laws, the world's moral ecosystems erode just as quickly and with equally devastating results. In times such as these, I can understand why it's difficult for some to imagine a future age when the earth will be restored, when disease will be all but eliminated, when there will be no pornography, no drunkenness, no drug addiction, and when lives will be so lengthened that a one-hundred-year-old person shall be considered a mere child (Isaiah 65:20). However, my friend, *we are ever so close to such an age*—the literal thousand-year reign of Jesus Christ on earth.

> Since the concept of a spatial city is both rational and intelligible because of twentieth-century space spectaculars, it is not difficult to imagine the impending advent of the Holy City.

A CITY HOVERING IN SPACE

As believers, we often focus so intently on the Tribulation events that lead to the return of Jesus to earth that we overlook or misunderstand the volumes of biblical references that refer to the most exciting, glorious, and fulfilling time in the history of our world—the period known as the Millennium. On occasion, my wife, Rexella, and I will receive a letter from a television viewer who writes something such as, "With all due respect, I do not believe that the subject of the Millennium is relevant for us as Christians today. After all, we will be raptured out of the world before the Tribulation period. Is not the Millennial age only for those individuals who survive Armageddon and for their offspring?" Well, with equally *due respect,* I must profoundly disagree. Those of us who will be taken out of this world, never experiencing death, will, uniquely, witness and be a significant part of the Millennial age. What do I mean by this statement? Jude, verse 14, teaches that we will return with Christ and then, during this thousand-year period, live in a spatial *city hovering above the earthly city of Jerusalem,* watching and interacting with the world below. That's right. I have not lost my marbles. And I did not pull that statement from a *Star Trek* television script. This is exactly what the Bible says. I know it may sound strange—a city, the New Jerusalem, just hanging out there in space. I remember when, as a teenager, I first read about this city in Revelation 21:2 and 21:10. I thought, *That can't be—a city hanging in space? How weird! How impossible!* Then, in 1969, our astronauts went to the moon and landed on the solid ground of another planet that was "hanging in space."

From that location the astronauts looked at the earth and discovered it also was "hanging in space." So, in effect, the earth itself—spinning at a rate of 25,000 miles per day—is a world suspended in space and upheld by the power of our God and Savior, the Lord Jesus Christ (Hebrews 1:3). Since the concept of a spatial city is both rational and intelligible because of twentieth-century space spectaculars, it is not difficult to imagine the impending advent of the Holy City.

The "New Jerusalem" is a city so bright that its glow will light the world both by day and by night. It is where we will live in new spiritual bodies that allow us to walk through walls, disappear and reappear at will, and travel at the speed of our own desires, just as Jesus did in His resurrection body (Luke 24:36-41). Do you remember how the disciples recognized the Lord after He rose from the grave? Do you remember how they could touch Him and feel His flesh and bones? Do you recall how Jesus went out and did some fishing, prepared a meal for His followers, and ate with them? This same Jesus was seen in His resurrection body by between 500 to 1,000 people, according to eyewitness accounts (1 Corinthians 15:3-8). And what makes us think that we will be like Jesus after the Rapture? The Word of God. According to 1 Thessalonians 4:16-17, when "the dead in Christ shall rise first: Then we which are alive and remain shall be caught up together with them in the clouds, to meet the Lord in the air." Then we're told in 1 Corinthians 15:52 that it will all occur "in the twinkling of an eye," and as we sweep through heavens one and two, we will be changed to be like Jesus (Philippians 3:21; 1 John 3:2). The psalmist wrote in Psalm 17:15: "I shall be satisfied, when I awake, with thy likeness." First John 3:2 adds: "When he shall appear, we shall be like him."

> **Satan will be bound in chains during this period, but the world will not be without temptation as the people of this era will still be partakers of an old sinful nature.**

AN EARTH LIKE NOTHING IN THE PAST

Like Jesus, housed in spirit bodies, we will be able to see, touch, partake of food, and *co-mingle with the humans on earth* (Luke 24:39-42). We will be able to move across the universe at the speed of thought. Even more exciting, we will live in that new Holy City, the New Jerusalem that hovers over the globe in the Millennial era. Meanwhile, there will be people down below—on earth— living in their human bodies under the personal rule of Jesus. They will be involved with others socially, economically, physically, and politically. However, it will be a very different world from the one you and I know today. There will be peace with justice. Death will occur, but life will be greatly extended—*especially for those who abstain from sin.* Satan will be bound in chains during this period, but the world will not be without temptation as the people of this era will still be partakers of an old sinful nature. This is why their children will rebel at the conclusion of the Millennium (Revelation 20:8-9). Sin will be greatly reduced, *but it will still be a part of this new world,* and, in fact, the degree of people's transgressions will determine how brief or how long they live. But how is sin possible if Satan is bound and Christ rules the world with a rod of iron? James expounds this issue clearly in chapter 1 verses 13-15: "Let no man say when he is tempted, I am tempted of God: for God cannot be tempted with evil, neither tempteth he any man: But every man is tempted, when he is drawn away of his own lust, and enticed. Then when lust hath conceived, it bringeth forth sin: and sin, when it is finished, bringeth forth death."

In that glorious day vice will be virtually unknown because Christ will not allow it. There will be a *zero-tolerance* attitude toward evil. In Revelation 19:15, we read—and we've mentioned this often—that the Lord will rule the world "with a rod of iron." That is the critical difference between now and then. Jesus will return to earth as a benevolent dictator, and the world will operate under a true theocracy. Today, we think of a theocracy as a government ruled by a church or religious figure. But the root word, *theos,* means "God." So the Millennium will truly see the world ruled exclusively by

Christ. Suddenly the prayer that Jesus instructed us to pray, "Thy kingdom come. Thy will be done in earth, as it is in heaven," will take on new significance. Although we will not experience complete righteousness until *after* the Millennial Kingdom, this period will literally see the Lord's will done *on earth as it is in heaven*. However, to make this happen, Christ must break stubborn, carnal wills (Psalm 2:9). After all, those who inhabit the earth during the Millennium will be much like people today. They will still bear children who possess Adamic natures (Romans 5:12). Therefore, by the end of the Millennial age, many of the offspring of godly parents will become rebellious. That's right—when Satan is unleashed before the final judgment, multitudes of these rebels actually will join forces with the devil. During the Millennium, people will remain under control for one reason alone: Jesus will be there to break their stubborn natures with His "rod of iron." Without that force, chaos would reign because the wickedness of the human heart refuses to change. Thus, without the presence of Satan, people will go astray because of their fleshly desires. All humanity will enter the Millennium period righteous and repentant. But believers will bear children who turn away from their parents and God. Imagine—after living under Christ's authority for one thousand years, they will still become like Judas Iscariot and revolt against the Lord.

As promised, Jesus will come again and rule the world. That time, my friend, is at hand and may be very soon.

WHY ARE THERE STILL DOUBTERS?

Yet, with all this information about the Millennium, one thing continues to bring pain to my heart. Millions of believers still doubt the reality of the coming physical and spiritual rule of Christ. However, to disbelieve that Jesus will reign on earth for one thousand years is literally to rip whole passages from the Bible. Hundreds of verses back up the reality of this period. Here is just a handful of such references with which to begin your own personal study: Psalm 2:6: "I have set my king upon my holy hill of Zion." Zechariah 14:2-9: here we see all the armies of the world moving against Jerusalem as the Lord returns to set foot upon the Mount of Olives and begin His earthly reign as well as stop mankind from destroying one another and the earth (Revelation 11:18). Let's continue. "And the LORD shall be king over all the earth: in that day shall there be one LORD, and his name one" (Zechariah 14:9). (Notice the use of the word *day*, which in biblical terms often means one thousand years—Psalm 90:4; 2 Peter 3:8.) Both the Old and New Testaments refer clearly and frequently to this period in history—to Christ's return and His thousand-year reign. God is sovereign. He keeps His promises. And, as promised, Jesus will come again and rule the world. That time, my friend, is at hand and may be very soon.

With that as prologue, what will be the physical, economic, social, and "relational" aspects of the Millennium? How will people live? What will be the "stuff" of life? These are relevant questions because, remember, we who will have been raptured will be *hovering in heavens one and two over the earthly city of Jerusalem,* interacting with the people of earth—yet another reason to engage in a biblically based study of coming attractions. Let's look at some of the various aspects of Millennial life for those who live under the rule of Christ.

EARTH'S GOLDEN AGE

Christ's physical reign during the Millennium will precipitate such universal spiritual blessing that it will impact all aspects of life on planet earth. We have already observed how Christ's rule will produce righteousness and holy living. Isaiah 35:8 states: "And an highway shall be there, and a way, and it shall be called The way of holiness; the unclean shall not pass over it; but it shall be for those: the wayfaring men, though fools, shall not err therein." What does this verse mean? Simply that in contrast to previous generations, Christ's Millennial rule of righteousness will create the kind of environment that

will produce godliness and justice. Yes, holiness, righteousness, joy, and peace will be the hallmarks of Christ's
rule, with the standard of quasi-spiritual life far exceeding the spiritual enlightenment of any previous dispensation in history.

> War and human destruction have heretofore been the
> perennial scourge of human history, but when peace
> and justice arrive under the reign of Christ, war and
> bloodshed shall cease.

UNIVERSAL PEACE AND JUSTICE

The fact that wars will no longer be fought during
the Millennium will have a profound and salutary effect
on the social, political, and economic life of the world.
There will be no more expenditure for massive weapons
of destruction; the arms industry will go bust. War and
human destruction have heretofore been the perennial
scourge of human history, but when peace and justice
arrive under the reign of Christ, war and bloodshed
shall cease. Every soldier since the beginning of history
has known that war is hell, that war is the enemy of life,
well-being, happiness, and optimism. The effect of war
on the lives of individuals and the communities in which
they live has been the bane of our existence. World War
I destroyed at least ten million people in battle, most of
them young, as well as millions more from battle-related

causes. World War II destroyed fifty million, of whom fewer than half were servicemen and women in uniform. Yugoslavia, for example, lost 10 percent of its population, of which but a fraction belonged to the Royal Yugoslav Army; the rest died through deprivation or internecine massacre. The toll of World War II persisted well beyond the great peace of 1945. Civil war and wars of national liberation, in Korea, Vietnam, Algeria, the Middle East, Iran, Iraq, Angola, and Mozambique, and the interethnic wars that have followed the dissolution of empires, are often calculated to have killed another 50 million. And the blitzkrieg continues. How conscious we also are of the massive bloodshed in this decade, such as the slaughter in Rwanda and Bosnia that has added another million or more victims to the century's casualty list. If the price of war were measured strictly in statistics, it could perhaps be shrugged off. The cost, however, cannot be measured on graphs alone. The unquantifiable cost is in emotional suffering, by which the pain of one death is multiplied many times over through the network of family relationships and in long-term, lifelong deprivation.

Under Christ's reign, this sorry litany of history will be just that—history. For during the thousand-year reign of our Savior, money once used for armaments will be redirected to improving the world in a myriad of ways. Oppressive taxation will be relieved, the economy will be freed up, and the Dow will go, undoubtedly, to even dizzier heights. (As I write these words, it has just hit 11,000.) Couple this economic renewal during the Millennium with universal justice, assuring minorities of their "fair shake," more government protection, and greater economic opportunities, and it will indeed look like a brand-new world. Psalm 72 speaks eloquently to these profoundly different Millennial conditions:

> Give the king thy judgments, O God, and thy right-eousness unto the king's son. He shall judge thy people with righteousness, and thy poor with judgment. The mountains shall bring peace to the people, and the little hills, by righteousness. He shall judge the poor of the people, he shall save the children of the needy, and shall break in pieces the oppressor. They shall fear thee as long as the sun and moon endure, throughout all generations. He shall come down like rain upon the mown grass: as showers that water the earth. In his days shall the righteous flourish; and abundance of peace so long as the moon endureth. He shall have dominion also from sea to sea, and from the river unto the ends of the earth. They that dwell in the wilderness shall bow before him; and his enemies shall lick the dust. The kings of Tarshish and of the isles shall bring presents: the kings of Sheba and Seba shall offer gifts. Yea, all kings shall fall down before him: all nations shall serve him. For he shall deliver the needy when he crieth; the poor also, and him that hath no helper. He

shall spare the poor and needy, and shall save the souls of the needy. He shall redeem their soul from deceit and violence: and precious shall their blood be in his sight. And he shall live, and to him shall be given of the gold of Sheba: prayer also shall be made for him continually; and daily shall he be praised. There shall be an handful of corn in the earth upon the top of the mountains; the fruit thereof shall shake like Lebanon: and they of the city shall flourish like grass of the earth. His name shall endure for ever: his name shall be continued as long as the sun: and men shall be blessed in him: all nations shall call him blessed. Blessed be the LORD God, the God of Israel, who only doeth wondrous things. And blessed be his glorious name for ever: and let the whole earth be filled with his glory; Amen, and Amen. The prayers of David the son of Jesse are ended.

> **Within a short time, all our present ecological disasters will be turned around, and this turnaround will happen because Christ brings with Him *a time of restitution.***

ADAM'S CURSE IS LIFTED

Another key ingredient that will contribute to the Millennium's "new way of doing business" will be the elimination of the curse of Adam's sin. In Genesis 3, God cursed the earth because of Adam's iniquity. Now, when Christ returns, that terrible curse will be lifted. Therefore, we will see the flourishing of vegetation such as we have never witnessed before. Within a short time, all our present ecological disasters will be turned around, and this turnaround will happen because Christ brings with Him *a time of restitution* (Acts 3:21). Amazingly, within a few years of Christ's rule on earth, everything will be changed. Isaiah writes,

> The wilderness and the solitary place shall be glad for them; and the desert shall rejoice, and blossom as the rose. It shall blossom abundantly, and rejoice even with joy and singing: the glory of Lebanon shall be given unto it, the excellency of Carmel and Sharon, they shall see the glory of the LORD, and the excellency of our God. Strengthen ye the weak hands, and confirm the feeble knees. Say to them that are of a fearful heart, Be strong, fear not: behold, your God will come with vengeance, even God with a recompence; he will come and save you. Then the eyes of the blind shall be opened, and the ears of the deaf shall be unstopped. Then shall the lame man leap as an hart, and the tongue of the dumb sing: for in the wilderness shall waters break out, and streams in the desert (Isaiah 35:1-6).

What a difference from the kind of earth you and I live in today. The TV weathermen during the Millennium will have a job that borders on boredom, since universal rainfall will be abundant. It will be the same good news night after night. And what about the fate of cattle and the vital availability of food? Again, Isaiah gives us this information when he writes, "Then shall he give the rain of thy seed, that thou shalt sow the ground withal; and bread of the increase of the earth, and it shall be fat and plenteous: in that day shall thy cattle feed in large pastures. The oxen likewise and the young asses that ear the ground shall eat clean provender, which hath been winnowed with the shovel and with the fan" (Isaiah 30:23-24). Since death will continue to exist during the Millennium, we can assume that Adam's curse will only be partly lifted, at least until the new heaven and new earth become eternally part of the spiritual landscape after the thousand years (Revelation 22:3, 5). However, in general, it is safe to say that the world will be in the best shape ever as it is delivered from nonproductivity, greed, and avarice into an era of unprecedented bounty and prosperity.

> This overall sense of well-being will result in an era of prosperity such as humankind has never known.

PROSPERITY WILL ABOUND

You will undoubtedly remember that the brave, experimental pilots who inspired the film *The Right Stuff* were known for their lack of fear and their strong desire to challenge the limits of space and for their own capacity to endure those limits. They were unafraid to fly higher, faster, and to push the envelope to new heights. They were free to think "out of the box," to think courageous thoughts, all attitudes that made them the heroes they ultimately became. Keep these examples in mind as you think of how the people of the Millennium will suddenly be able to function in their own highly charged environment of freedom, peace, and justice. They will attempt new ventures and will, under Christ's rule of iron, begin practicing righteousness and holiness as they find themselves suddenly set free from Satan's temptations. His imprisonment for the entire one thousand years guarantees this. Here are some passages that describe how this abundance will manifest itself: Jeremiah 31:12 says, "Their soul shall be as a watered garden; and they shall not sorrow any more at all." We read in Ezekiel 34:25-26, "And I will make with them a covenant of peace, and will cause the evil beasts to cease out of the land: and they shall dwell safely in the wilderness, and sleep in the woods. And I will make them and the places round about my hill a blessing; and I will cause the shower to come down in his season; there shall be showers of blessing." This good news of Millennial prosperity is further advanced by Joel when he writes,

Fear not, O land; be glad and rejoice: for the LORD will do great things. Be not afraid, ye beasts of the field: for the pastures of the wilderness do spring, for the tree beareth her fruit, the fig tree and the vine do yield their strength. Be glad then, ye children of Zion, and rejoice in the LORD your God: for he hath given you the former rain moderately, and he will cause to come down for you the rain, the former rain, and the latter rain in the first month. And the floors shall be full of wheat, and the vats shall overflow with wine and oil. And I will restore to you the years that the locust hath eaten, the cankerworm, and the caterpiller, and the palmerworm, my great army which I sent among you. And ye shall eat in plenty, and be satisfied, and praise the name of the LORD your God, that hath dealt wondrously with you: and my people shall never be ashamed. And ye shall know that I am in the midst of Israel, and that I am the LORD your God, and none else: and my people shall never be ashamed (Joel 2:21-27).

And finally, from the book of Amos,

Behold, the days come, saith the LORD, that the plowman shall overtake the reaper, and the treader of grapes him that soweth seed; and the mountains shall drop sweet wine [grape juice], and all the hills shall melt. And I will bring again the captivity of my people of Israel, and they shall build the waste cities, and inhabit them; and they shall plant vineyards, and drink the wine [grape juice] thereof; they shall also make gardens, and eat the fruit of them (Amos 9:13-14).

Today the instrumental factors in creating physical and spiritual poverty for millions, such as an unequal distribution of goods, prejudice, avarice, hate, and personal and corporate distress, will be virtually nonexistent during the thousand-year reign of Christ. Placards of protest will be put aside as labor and management see eye to eye for the first time; there will be equal pay for equal work, and the "glass ceiling" that has kept women from climbing the steep ladder to business success will become a thing of the past. Isaiah sums up the spirit of these future days when he reminds us,

And they shall build houses, and inhabit them; and they shall plant vineyards, and eat the fruit of them. They shall not build, and another inhabit; they shall not plant, and another eat: for as the days of a tree are the days of my people, and mine elect shall long enjoy the work of their hands. They shall not labour in vain, nor bring forth for trouble; for they are the seed of the blessed of the LORD, and their offspring with them. And it shall come to pass, that before they call, I will answer; and while they are yet speaking, I will hear. The wolf and the lamb shall feed together, and the lion shall eat straw like the bullock: and dust shall be the serpent's meat. They shall not hurt nor

destroy in all my holy mountain, saith the LORD.
(Isaiah 65:21-25)

SICKNESS NO MORE

I would encourage you to pick up your Bible and begin to review the many times Jesus looked in compassion at desperately needy, physically sick people *and healed them.* He healed lepers, cast out demons from the deranged, raised the dead, and brought light to sightless eyes. However, all the drama of Jesus' healing ministry during His first advent will be nothing compared to the health, healing, and well-being that will be hallmarks of the Millennium. Again, we turn to Isaiah who writes, "And the inhabitant shall not say, I am sick: the people that dwell therein shall be forgiven their iniquity" (Isaiah 33:24). What an interesting thought and fascinating correlation between physical sickness and sin. And what about those without sight or hearing? Isaiah 35:5-6 declares: "Then the eyes of the blind shall be opened, and the ears of the deaf shall be unstopped. Then shall the lame man leap as an hart, and the tongue of the dumb sing: for in the wilderness shall waters break out, and streams in the desert."

However, not only will illness vanish from people's lives. Those with broken hearts will be healed (Isaiah 61:1-3). Long, healthy lives will be commonplace; there will be an exponential increase in the birthrate as children are born to parents who survived the terrors of the Great Tribulation. Every aspect of the Millennium will be positive, uplifting, affirming. It will truly be earth's "golden age"—the kind of utopia longed for by humankind throughout history. The dreams of all our social and religious reformers will suddenly become reality, but not through the efforts of humans pulling themselves up by their own bootstraps. During the Millennium, this change will come about through the all-encompassing, ever-present power, grace, and majesty of Christ Himself. And what a glorious day it will be.

I have just received the following commentary on our times from a friend of our ministry. These statements clearly demonstrate the kind of environment in which we live today. But keep in mind that Christ's rule during the Millennium will make such thinking obsolete:

> The paradox of our generation is that we have taller buildings, but shorter tempers; wider freeways, but narrower viewpoints; we spend more but enjoy it less. We have bigger houses and smaller families; more conveniences, but less time; we have more degrees, but less sense; more knowledge, but less judgment; more experts, but more problems; more medicine, but less health.
>
> We have multiplied our possessions, but reduced our values.
>
> We talk too much, love too seldom, and hate too often.

We've learned how to make a living, but not a life.

We've added years to life, not life to years.

We've been all the way to the moon and back, but have trouble crossing the street to meet a new neighbor.

We've conquered outer space, but not inner peace.

We've cleaned up the air, but polluted the soul.

We've split the atom, but not our prejudice.

We write more, but learn less.

We plan more, but accomplish less.

We've learned to rush, but not to wait.

We have higher incomes, but lower morals.

We've become long on quantity, but short on quality.

These are days of two incomes, but times of spiritual poverty.

Days of fancier houses, but broken homes.

These are days of quick trips, disposable diapers, throwaway morality, one-night stands, overweight bodies, and pills that do everything but produce joy.

This is how life on planet earth is for you and me today. However, during the Millennial reign of our Savior and Lord Jesus Christ, all things will become new. And, my friend, that time is coming soon.

For as the new heavens and the new earth, which I will make, shall remain before me, saith the LORD, so shall your seed and your name remain.
(Isaiah 66:22)

CHAPTER 9

THE HEAVENLY
JERUSALEM

T o develop a fuller understanding of this chapter, I encourage you to open your Bible to Revelation 21:9 to 22:21, and then please keep these references close at hand because, in my experience during fifty years of ministry, I've discovered there are few areas of God's Word that cut such a wide swath of differing opinion and interpretation. The primary issue is that some scholars see this passage as the definitive description of the heavenly city, or the New Jerusalem; others say these verses refer to the Church in relation to Christ, while still others suggest they speak solely to the nation of Israel and her relationship to the Messiah. For some, the heavenly Jerusalem is literally a city; others see it as a mere symbolic representation. In this book we espouse the view that the heavenly Jerusalem is a real city, peopled with real glorified bodies who interact with earth's inhabitants during the Millennial period. These are the primary issues at stake. However, rather than delve into the conflicting positions of opposing views, we will direct our attention to the scriptural position of the heavenly Jerusalem, a real place hovering above the earth during the thousand-year reign of our Lord Jesus Christ.

Dr. John F. Walvoord, in his landmark book *The Millennial Kingdom,* confirms the pre-Millennial position of the physical existence of the heavenly Jerusalem when he writes, "It may be demonstrated from Scripture that (1) the heavenly Jerusalem is the eternal habitation of all resurrected saints; (2) the heavenly Jerusalem is in existence in the millennium; (3) the Scriptures teach that there is some participation of these resurrected saints in the government of the millennium; (4) objections to comingling of resurrected with nonresurrected beings are unjustified."[1]

> Another city hovers above Jerusalem called the Holy City or the New Jerusalem.

THE TWO JERUSALEMS

A point of clarification is important at the outset. When we speak of "Jerusalem" in the study of Bible prophecy, we need to remember that we are referring to *two* Jerusalems: the city that exists in the Holy Land and the New Jerusalem that hovers over the earth. Same name, two entities. Now the Jerusalem "on earth" is the city captured by the Jews in 1967, an event prophesied in Luke 21:24 as one of the signs that Christ's return is at hand. On the other hand, another city hovers above Jerusalem called the Holy City or the New Jerusalem. In Revelation 21:10-11 we read, "And he carried me away in the spirit to a great and high mountain, and shewed me that great city, the holy Jerusalem, descending out of heaven from God, Having the glory of God: and her light was like unto a stone most precious, even like a jasper stone, clear as crystal." Revelation 22:5 adds, "And there shall be no night there; and they need no candle, neither light of the sun; for the Lord God giveth them light: and they shall reign for ever and ever." This is the place—the suspended city over the "earthly Jerusalem"—where God's raptured people, those who returned with Christ, dwell (Jude 14). It is a city where "the nations of them which are saved [on earth] shall walk in the light of it: and the kings of the earth do bring their glory and honour into it. And the gates of it shall not be shut at all by day: for there shall be no night there" (Revelation 21:24-25).

> On that glorious day when we arrive in the New Jerusalem, we will not only be with our Lord, but will also be able to enjoy meals and fellowship with Him.

PHYSICAL BODIES ON EARTH AND GLORIFIED BODIES IN THE HOLY CITY

So we observe two Jerusalems: the heavenly Jerusalem for those with new, translated bodies *that are unable to sin,* and the earthly Jerusalem where the inhabitants still have fleshly weaknesses because of possessing old Adamic natures that are able to sin. Let me expand this thought.

As Christians, we believe that Christ died for our sins, He was buried, and He rose again the third day according to the Scriptures (1 Corinthians 15:3-4). However, there is much more to this exciting story. Christ in His new, resurrected body—a spiritual entity—is, nevertheless, visible. He was seen by Cephas, then by the twelve, and after that by more than five hundred brethren at one time. Then James saw Him, next all the apostles, and finally Paul saw Him. Some five hundred to one thousand people saw Christ in His new spiritual body—a body that could materialize. Jesus also appeared to His disciples in Luke 24:39 when He amazed them by saying He was real: "Behold my hands and my feet, that it is I, myself: handle me, and see; for a spirit hath not flesh and bones, as ye see me have." In verse 41, Christ asks if they have any food. They do, and they give Him a piece of broiled fish and a honeycomb. He takes and eats it in front of them, signifying that a spiritual body still partakes of and enjoys the delicacies of life.

What a preview of coming attractions for the believer, for on that glorious day when we arrive in the New Jerusalem, we will not only be *with* our Lord, but we will also be able to enjoy meals and fellowship with Him. That's because you and I will have bodies like our Savior's. You will remember that Jesus could go through walls with His spirit body. Well, we know through recent scientific papers that the same is possible for all humans *if we learn to rearrange the molecules within the body*. So none of this is absurd. It is not even wild speculation. It is entirely possible that in our glorified bodies we'll move freely and swiftly, defying present-day physics.

Remember that the next major event on God's prophetic clock will be the Rapture, that moment when all believers will heed the call to "come up hither" (Revelation 4:1). We know the dead in Christ shall rise first, and then we who are alive and remain shall be caught up together in the clouds with the dead to meet our Lord in the air (1 Thessalonians 4:16-17). This will all happen in the twinkling of an eye (1 Corinthians 15:51-52). As we sweep through the heavenlies to meet our Savior, we will be changed to be like Him, for at that moment we will receive glorified bodies. David the psalmist said, "I shall be satisfied, when I awake, with thy likeness" (Psalm 17:15). In Philippians 3:21, Paul adds that Christ will change our vile bodies so they might be fashioned like His own glorious body. That's why 1 John 3:2 states that when we see

Jesus, "we shall be like him; for we shall see him as he is." What a glorious day that will be.

> We will not be lonely in our new dwelling, for we *will* have the capacity to co-mingle and to coexist with the people on earth as well as the saints in the glorious Holy City.

NO LONGER SCIENCE FICTION

Imagine! We will be able to do what our Savior was able to do. In our magnificent *spirit bodies* we will be seen, we will be able to touch others and be touched, and we will be able to vanish at will and reappear just as readily. At long last, we will be able to do *in practice* what scientists have only theorized for years. Yes, we will be able to penetrate walls and move instantaneously through many dimensions. All this may become a glorious reality soon. This is *not* science fiction. It is a faithful promise from the heart of God. Did you know that we will be able to travel as *fast as thought?* Not long ago, scientists discovered yet another quasar, the farthest from earth yet to be observed. Try to fathom this: The quasar in question is 70 trillion billion miles from earth. Now that is a long, long way from home—farther even than where ET lives! However, there is something even more remarkable. You and I, as dwellers in the New Jerusalem hovering above the earth, will be able to move trillions of miles in a split second—as fast as thought—because we shall have bodies like our Lord's. Furthermore, we will not be lonely in our new dwelling, for we will have the capacity to co-mingle and coexist with the people on earth as well as the saints in the glorious Holy City. And the best news of all—our comings and goings will be traversed like a bolt of lightning. Just as Jesus in His new body (Luke 24:39) was able to co-mingle and do what He did with His disciples, so will it be possible for celestial and terrestrial bodies tethered to earth to interact (1 Corinthians 15). I can only imagine the stories that will emerge from such encounters.

A LITERAL CITY

This spinning, heavenly city is for real, and at the appointed time, believers will become inhabitants of this sublime, celestial place. First, during the one-thousand-year reign of Christ as it hovers over the earth, as announced in Revelation 21:9–22:15, then eternally as this heavenly palace descends to earth and becomes situated on terra firma as recorded in Revelation 21:1-8. Let's investigate.

> And I saw a new heaven and a new earth: for the first heaven and the first earth were passed away; and there was no more sea. And I John saw the holy city, new Jerusalem, coming down from God out of heaven,

prepared as a bride adorned for her husband. And I heard a great voice out of heaven saying, Behold, the tabernacle of God is with men, and he will dwell with them, and they shall be his people, and God himself shall be with them, and be their God (Revelation 21:1-3).

The heavenly Jerusalem is the eternal habitation of our Lord God. It will also be the capital of the New Creation. Built into its very foundations are the glory and majesty of God (Revelation 21:11, 23; 22:5). Within its boundaries will be housed the great throne of the Almighty. "And there shall be no more curse: but the throne of God and of the Lamb shall be in it; and his servants shall serve him" (Revelation 22:3). It will be a place of intimacy with God. He will see us and know us, for we shall see His face in this city of splendor that will be the place of God's abode for all time to come. Revelation 22:5b tells us, "And they shall reign for ever and ever." This will follow the thousand-year reign of Christ when our Lord will be recommissioned to continue eternally His reign on earth (Revelation 11:15), and we will also be allowed to continue with Him in ruling the world for all eternity.

What a joyous announcement: *The Bride has come; be prepared to shout with joy at her entrance.*

DWELLING PLACE OF THE BRIDE, DESTINY OF THE CHURCH

Revelation 21:9-10 says, "And there came unto me one of the seven angels which had the seven vials full of the seven last plagues, and talked with me, saying, Come hither, I will shew thee the Bride, the Lamb's wife. And he carried me away in the spirit to a great and high mountain, and shewed me that great city, the holy Jerusalem, descending out of heaven from God." I hope you are becoming as excited as I am as we work through the intricacies of life in the New Jerusalem, especially when we realize that an angel reveals this city to be the location of the Bride, the Lamb's wife. What a joyous announcement: *The Bride has come; be prepared to shout with joy at her entrance.* And what else might we discover in this heavenly place? Hear the word of the Lord from Hebrews 12:22-23: "But ye are come unto mount Sion, and unto the city of the living God, the heavenly Jerusalem, and to an innumerable company of angels, To the general assembly and church of the firstborn, which are written in heaven, and to God the Judge of all, and to the spirits of just men made perfect." These two verses speak eloquently of the promise that the heavenly Jerusalem is the ultimate destiny of the Church, also called Christ's Bride. This truth is further affirmed in Revelation 3:12 where we read, "Him that overcometh will I make a pillar in the temple of my God, and he shall go no more out: and I will write upon him the name of my God, and the name of the city of my God, which is new Jerusalem, which cometh down out of heaven from my God: and I will write upon him my new name." New Jerusalem. New name. New people. New life. This is surely the place Jesus referred to in John 14:1-3, "Let not your heart be troubled: ye believe in God, believe also in me. In my Father's house are many mansions: if it were not so, I would have told you. I go to prepare a place for you. And if I go and prepare a place for you, I will come again, and receive you unto myself; that where I am, there ye may be also."

My friend, has the significance of all this hit you yet? You, as a believer, will be an active, joyous participant in the activities of the heavenly Jerusalem, a city inhabited by the eternal God and by those who have been redeemed by the blood of the spotless, sinless Lamb.

ENTRANCE TO THE NEW JERUSALEM

How will we make our entrance through the city's portals? In only two ways: through the Rapture of the Church and by resurrection. Once the judgment seat of Christ and the marriage of the Lamb have been accomplished, the Lamb—the Bride of Christ—makes the New Jerusalem her final, eternal home. However, since the resurrection of the redeemed of Israel occurs at the Second Coming of Christ, it is impossible for the "saved of Israel" to enter the Holy City until *after* their resurrection (Daniel 12:2). The great prophecy scholar and teacher J. Dwight Pentecost writes, "Living Israel and living Gentiles on the earth at the second advent do not enter this city, but they enter the millennial reign of Christ. The same Old Testament saints, who are looking for the city with foundations, enter this city by resurrection. Thus all the redeemed of the ages who enter the city do so by resurrection. The city thus becomes the abode of all the resurrected saints, who enter it at the time of their resurrection."[2] And what of this city's relationship to the Millennial age? Again, Dr. Pentecost,

When the church has been joined in marriage to the Bridegroom and is installed in her prepared place she will never be moved out of it again. The church enters her eternal state at the rapture. When the Lord returns with His bride to reign, her dwelling place is not to be left unoccupied for a thousand years. Rather, the place of occupancy is transferred from heaven to a position over the earth. Thus John sees the "great city, the holy Jerusalem, descending out of heaven from God." This dwelling place remains in the air, to cast its light, which is the shining of the effulgence of the Son, onto the earth so that "the nations of them which are saved shall walk in the light of it: and the kings of the earth do bring their glory and honour into it" (Revelation 21:24). At the second advent, the time of the descent of the city into the air over the earth, the church saints are joined by the

Old Testament and Tribulation saints, who are resurrected and who take up residence at that time.[3]

LIFE WITHOUT END IN THE
NEW JERUSALEM

I wish I could give you a detailed account of how life
will be lived in this heavenly city, but unfortunately there
is no such specific information within the pages of
Scripture. We can only read with care the inspired words
of God's manifesto to determine what lies behind the
divine expression of life in the New Jerusalem. Although
not privy to details, we can surmise the following:

Life with the Lamb in the New Jerusalem will be . . .

- **A life of eternal service.** Many believers on earth
  have, with God's help and in His strength, done
  their best to serve God and their fellow citizens during their span of days on earth. However, in the
  New Jerusalem, there will be a service to God as
  never before, as proclaimed in Revelation 22:3,
  which states: "The throne of God and of the Lamb
  shall be in it; and his servants shall serve him." We
  are those servants!

There will be no evil, no sin, no gossip, no filth, and
no iniquity of any kind.

- **A life of righteousness.** There will be no evil, no sin, no gossip, no filth, and no iniquity of any kind because "there shall in no wise enter into it any thing that defileth, neither whatsoever worketh abomination, or maketh a lie: but they which are written in the Lamb's book of life" (Revelation 21:27).

- **A time of rest from our labor.** Many of us grew up listening to the plaintive song "Peace in the Valley." Well, in the New Jerusalem, there will be more than peace in the valley. There will be peace everywhere, and it will be a peace and repose that lasts forever. John writes, "And I heard a voice from heaven saying unto me, Write, Blessed are the dead which die in the Lord from henceforth: Yea, saith the Spirit, that they may rest from their labours; and their works do follow them" (Revelation 14:13).

- **A life of bounty and abundance.** The spirit of poverty and the debilitating terror of want will be absent from life in the Holy City, and we will eternally enjoy the delicacies of life (Revelation 22:2).

- **A life of glory and worship.** We will finally be done with the troubles and heartaches experienced in today's world. While we once looked through a glass darkly, as earthlings, we now see our Savior face to face. Once we lived by faith; now we live by sight. Though it was a struggle on earth as we, God's people, experienced bodily affliction, discouragement, pain, and distress, we persevered by faith because we knew that a new day was coming and that our suffering would be rewarded (James 1:12). This is confirmed by 2 Corinthians 4:17, "For our light affliction, which is but for a moment, *worketh for us a far more exceeding and eternal weight of glory*" (italics added). What we have endured on earth is minimal compared to the *weight of glory* that we'll share in the presence of the King of kings and Lord of lords in that rapidly approaching and glorious day.

And what about worship in the new, heavenly city? Worship will be a praise-a-thon such as none of us has ever known during our earthly sojourn. There will be nonstop services of adulation to the Lamb. That's the spectacular announcement of Revelation 7:9-12. I suggest that you read this text repeatedly until goose pimples begin to appear over your entire body. Read the words over and over again with joy, excitement, and anticipation, realizing, if one knows the Lord Jesus Christ, he or she will participate in this great, never-ending celestial celebration. And here's the exciting text:

> After this I beheld, and, lo, a great multitude, which no man could number, of all nations, and kindreds, and people, and tongues, stood before the throne, and before the Lamb, clothed with white robes, and palms

in their hands; And cried with a loud voice, saying, Salvation to our God which sitteth upon the throne, and unto the Lamb. And all the angels stood round about the throne, and about the elders and the four beasts, and fell before the throne on their faces, and worshipped God, Saying, Amen: Blessing, and glory, and wisdom, and thanksgiving, and honour, and power, and might, be unto our God for ever and ever. Amen (Revelation 7:9-12).

> On that great day, we will take the music from Handel's *Messiah* and sing it as we never could vocalize it on earth, even if we were in the finest choir, chorale, or musical group ever assembled.

In the heavenly Jerusalem, we will have the party of our lives, a soiree unlike anything we have ever known. However, our ultimate preoccupation will not just be our enjoyment of this great city and all it has to offer. Instead, the focus of our attention, the locus of our praise, and the center of our awareness will be the supreme glorification of our almighty Lord as we "see his face" (Revelation 22:4). In that day, we will give our undivided attention to the Lord of Glory, the One who loved us, gave Himself for us, washed us in His blood, and made us kings and priests unto God and His Father (Revelation 1:5-6). On that great day, we will take the music from Handel's *Messiah* and sing it as we never could vocalize it on earth, even if we were in the finest choir, chorale, or musical group ever assembled. We will lift our voices and lustily sing, "Worthy is the Lamb that was slain to receive power, and riches, and wisdom, and strength, and honour, and glory, and blessing" (Revelation 5:12).

Lord Jesus Christ . . .

Give us the strength to live our lives and pursue Your work as if Your coming was *but a moment away*. Increase our vision and fill us with compassion for those who do not know You, and stretch our minds to do all we can to bring the good news of the gospel of grace and the gospel of the coming kingdom to those who have ears to hear. May we seek to extend the boundaries of Your love, for Your Name's sake. We await Your coming, our gracious King. Maranatha.

And when the thousand years are expired, Satan shall
be loosed out of his prison, And shall go out to deceive
the nations which are in the four quarters of the earth,
Gog and Magog, to gather them together to battle: the
number of whom is as the sand of the sea.
And they went up on the breadth of the earth, and
compassed the camp of the saints about, and the
beloved city: and fire came down from God
out of heaven, and devoured them.
(Revelation 20:7-9, italics added)

CHAPTER 10

THE FINAL DAYS

❦

We now come to the great denouement of the plot, an unraveling of the final chapter of the story of all stories, the thousand years of Christ's reign on earth, ten centuries as no other. According to Revelation 20:7-9, at the end of the Millennium Satan will be freed from his bonds and will be permitted to work his mischief one more time as he has done throughout the ages. Scripture tells us that those duped by the great deceiver will be those born during the Millennial Kingdom by parents who entered the Kingdom in their Adamic, fleshly bodies and, therefore, are able to bear offspring with carnal natures. The thousand years of deprivation will not deter Satan from seeking those whom he may devour (1 Peter 5:8). As always, he will remain true to his vile nature, to the degree of again trying to usurp the place of God, demanding the allegiance, obedience, and worship from his followers that is due to God alone. A cliché says, "If you go to bed with dogs, you will wake up with fleas." This would be an appropriate comment for those would-be Christians who will join the forces of Satan at the close of the Millennium and who participate in the final, but futile, revolt against the almighty God, Jesus Christ our Lord. The evil of the devil will rub off on all who make Satan their comrade in arms, yet their forces will be formidable, their numbers so great that they will surround the city of Jerusalem as they prepare to do battle against the Lord of Hosts. These rebels will be individuals, political representatives, and rulers of regions and states—all harboring rebellion in their hearts. And what will be the outcome of this brash, last-gasp skirmish? Revelation 20:9b gives us the answer: "And fire came down from God out of heaven, and devoured them."

> The destruction of Satan and his minions will be final evidence that God judges sin to the bitter end.

THE DEMISE OF SATAN

Finally, at long last, Satan's work will be finished, and he will be cast unceremoniously into the lake of fire—the ultimate destiny of all who refuse to accept Jesus as their Savior and Lord—a place of eternal punishment inhabited by the beast, the false prophet, and all others who chose to go their way instead of the way of the Messiah (Revelation 20:10). There they will suffer torment day and night for ever and ever (Revelation 14:11). The destruction of Satan and his minions will be the final evidence that God judges sin to the bitter end. Satan will be the poster child for this reality as he burns in the fiery lake for eternity. Dr. Walvoord in his book *Major Bible Prophecies* makes this comment,

> A sad footnote is also indicated in this passage concerning the Beast and the False Prophet who as the world ruler and his associate will have been cast into the lake of fire a thousand years earlier. Here they will still be alive and in torment. "They will be tormented day and night for ever and ever" (Revelation 20:10) refers to Satan and the Beast and the False Prophet. Hard as it is for the human mind to contemplate unending torment, this is what the Bible teaches. Just as heaven goes on forever as a testimony to the grace of God, so the lake of fire will go on forever as a testimony to the righteousness of God. With the judgment of Satan and of those who joined with him in rebellion against God, the Millennium will come to a sudden close, paving the way for the dramatic scene of the new heaven and the new earth that follows.[1]

> The physical manifestation of His power will be seen in the establishment of the Great White Throne, in front of which will appear the great and the small, the known and the unknown.

THE JUDGMENT OF THE
GREAT WHITE THRONE

Revelation 20:11-15 is one of the most tragic passages in the Bible. After this season of violent rebellion on earth following the Millennium, we read,

And I saw a great white throne, and him that sat on it, from whose face the earth and the heaven fled away; and there was found no place for them. And I saw the dead, small and great, stand before God; and the books were opened: and another book was opened, which is the book of life: and the dead were judged out of those things which were written in the books, according to their works. And the sea gave up the dead which were in it; and death and hell delivered up the dead which were in them: and they were judged every man according to their works. And death and hell were cast into the lake of fire. This is the second death. And whosoever was not found written in the book of life was cast into the lake of fire.

These fateful words further indicate that God will not be mocked—not even by those who have lost their lives or had their cremated ashes deposited in the depths of the sea. There is no escaping the judgment of a holy God. The physical manifestation of His power will be seen in the establishment of the Great White Throne, in front of which will appear the great and the small, the known and the unknown. With heads bowed in shame, these unrepentant souls will then know that if any were not found written in the book of life, he or she would be cast into the lake of fire, referred to as the "second death." What a sad commentary for those who will have once had an opportunity to follow the Savior, but did not. Should this not give you and me pause, and cause us to reflect on both our obligation and privilege of sharing the good news with the lost, *today*, while there is yet time?

QUESTIONS AND ANSWERS

Over the years, Rexella and I have received literally thousands of letters that have asked specific, detailed questions about the significance of the Great White Throne Judgment. I have taken some time to organize the most often asked questions for your benefit, along with my response. Please use these for your own study, and share them with your friends. They are *that* important. You will notice that I will use the Word of God primarily to provide you with answers to these vital questions.

Q: Will all the wicked be resurrected for the Great White Throne Judgment?

A: Yes, definitely. This is clearly stated in John 5:28, 29, "For the hour is coming, in the which all that are in the graves shall hear his voice, And shall come forth; they that have done good, unto the resurrection of life; and they that have done evil, unto the resurrection of damnation." So, there are two resurrections—one unto life, which occurs at the Rapture, and the other unto damnation, coming at the raising of the dead for the final judgment. Acts 24:15 also declares, "There shall be a resurrection of the dead, both of the just and unjust."

Q: Who will be turned away from heaven at this judgment?

A: Revelation 21:8 and 22:15 describe those who will not be allowed to enter the Holy City, the New Jerusalem, which then descends from heaven, its former location, for one thousand years, and situates itself on earth forever. Who are excluded? "The fearful, and unbelieving, and the abominable, and murderers, and whoremongers, and sorcerers, and idolaters, and all liars, shall have their part in the lake which burneth with fire and brimstone: which is the second death. . . . For without [the Holy City] are dogs, and sorcerers, and whoremongers, and murderers, and idolaters, and whosoever loveth and maketh a lie." This description, combined with additional sins found in Romans 1:24-32 and 1 Corinthians 6:9-10, provides a comprehensive picture of those who are lost for all eternity:

- The fearful—those who do not accept Christ because they wish to escape being ridiculed (Matthew 10:32)

- Unbelievers—those who do not believe and receive the Lord Jesus Christ (John 8:24)

- The abominable—those who engage in wicked practices (Titus 1:16)

- Murderers (Galatians 5:19-21)

- Whoremongers—those who engage in fornication or consort with prostitutes (Ephesians 5:5-8; Hebrews 13:4)

- Sorcerers—those who practice witchcraft, demonism, and follow after the occult. This word comes from the Greek root word *pharmakeia* and means "enchantment with drugs." Thus, drug users, addicts, and even pushers (the Greek *pharmakeus*) are included in this category (Relevation 21:8)

- Idolaters—those who worship or revere anyone or anything other than the living and true God (Exodus 20:4-5; Psalm 115:4-8; 1 John 5:21)

- Liars (John 8:44)

- Dogs—false professors (2 Peter 2:22)

- The unrighteous—those who trust in self, in works, or in a false religious system, or mere "religion" for salvation (1 Corinthians 6:9-10; Titus 3:5)

- Fornicators—those who engage in premarital or extramarital sex, or promiscuity of any kind (Galatians 5:19-21)

- The wicked—those who disregard all morality and moral standards (Proverbs 14:12)

- The covetous—those who wish all things for themselves, especially things that belong to others (Ephesians 5:5-8)

- The malicious—those who willfully seek to destroy a person through gossip (James 1:26; James 3)

- The envious—those resentful of others (Romans 1:29-32)

- Deceivers—those who purposely mislead or betray others (2 Timothy 3:13)

- Whisperers—gossips (Romans 1:29)

- Haters of God (Romans 1:30)

- The spiteful—those who express hatred for others (1 John 3:15)

- The proud—those possessing an excessively high opinion of themselves (Proverbs 6:16-18)

- Boasters—those who exalt self (1 Timothy 3:6)

- Inventors of evil things (Romans 1:30)

- The disobedient to parents (Ephesians 6:1-3)

- Those without understanding (resulting from unconcern or rejection of the truth) (Romans 1:31-32)

- Covenant breakers—those who do not keep their word. (The Antichrist is the supreme example of this type of person [Daniel 9:27].)

- The implacable—those exhibiting extreme stubbornness to the point of refusing to yield to the convicting power of the Holy Spirit (Proverbs 1:24-28; Acts 7:51-52)

- The unmerciful—those who lack compassion (Ephesians 4:32)

- Adulterers—those who practice extramarital sex (Hebrews 13:4)

- The effeminate—those generally younger persons in the process of becoming hardened homosexuals or "sodomites" (Jude 7)

- Abusers of themselves with mankind—hardened homosexuals (Genesis 19:5)

- Thieves (1 Corinthians 6:9-10)

- Drunkards—those given to and overcome by alcohol (Proverbs 20:1; 23:20, 21; Luke 21:34; Romans 13:13; 1 Corinthians 6:10; Galatians 5:19-21; Ephesians 5:18)

- Revilers—those who use abusive or contemptuous language (1 Corinthians 6:9-10)

- Extortioners—those who exact money from, or take advantage of, others through violence, threats, or misuse of authority (1 Corinthians 5:9-11; 6:10)

As you can plainly see, sin does not pay. Galatians 6:7 states, "Be not deceived; God is not mocked: for whatsoever a man soweth, that shall he also reap."

Every member of the human race is a sinner—has missed the mark—and is guilty before God.

This occurs at the judgment of the Great White Throne when God opens the books and reveals the recorded deeds of the lost (Revelation 20:11-15).

But here is the greatest news ever! I would like to share one additional verse of Scripture, which reveals the heart and love of God—1 Corinthians 6:11, which states,

"And such were some of you: but ye are washed, but ye are sanctified, but ye are justified in the name of the Lord Jesus, and by the Spirit of our God." Oh, the transforming power of the blood of Christ which cleanseth us from all sin (1 John 1:7). Each member of the human race is a sinner—has missed the mark—and is guilty before God (Romans 3:23). Yet God has given every person a blessed way of escaping the condemnation due him. That's why Titus 2:11 declares that "the grace of God that bringeth salvation hath appeared to all men." Thus, "He that believeth on [Christ] is not condemned" (John 3:18).

Q: Who will be the judge at the Great White Throne Judgment?

A: None other than the person of our Lord Jesus Christ (Romans 2:16; John 5:27). Acts 17:31 adds, "He hath appointed a day, in the which he will judge the world in righteousness by that man whom he hath ordained; whereof he hath given assurance unto all men, in that he hath raised him [the judge] from the dead." The resurrected one is Jesus. Thus, Jesus will be the Judge and will judge righteously.

> God knows everything about us (Psalm 139:4). He even knows the minutest detail of our thought life (Ezekiel 11:5). He knows everything about everything and all things about all things.

Q: We have all heard the expression "God is keeping the books!" Is this really true? Does God keep a detailed record of each of us?

A: Yes! There is no doubt about it. God knows everything about us (Psalm 139:4). He even knows the minutest detail of our thought life (Ezekiel 11:5). He knows everything about everything and all things about all things. He is an accurate, meticulously thorough bookkeeper. In Psalm 139:1-4, 6, the psalmist speaks about what God knows about him and is shockingly amazed: "O LORD, thou hast searched me, and known me. Thou knowest my downsitting and mine uprising, thou understandest my thought afar off. Thou compassest my path and my lying down, and art acquainted with all my ways. For there is not a word in my tongue, but, lo, O LORD, thou knowest it altogether. . . . Such knowledge is too wonderful for me." This same magnificent, omniscient God keeps a record on you and me.

Q: What happens *following* the Great White Throne Judgment?

A: God refines this old world (Isaiah 48:10), and He creates something spectacular. "For, behold, I create new heavens and a new earth: and the former shall not be remembered, nor come into mind" (Isaiah 65:17). "And I saw a new heaven and a new earth: for the first heaven and the first earth were passed away; and there was no more sea. And I John saw the holy city, new Jerusalem, coming down from God out of heaven, prepared as a bride adorned for her husband" (Revelation 21:1-2). "And he carried me away in the spirit to a great and high mountain, and shewed me that great city, the holy Jerusalem, descending out of heaven from God" (Revelation 21:10). "Even so, come, Lord Jesus" (Revelation 22:20).

PEACE IN THE FINAL DAYS

My friend, we have now come to the end of this book that I have titled *Millennium: Beginning or End?* I trust you will agree that the title speaks accurately of this amazing, earth-changing period of one thousand years known as the Millennium, a day that is closer than most Christians dare to contemplate.

Are we there yet? No, not quite. However, with each tick of the prophetic clock, we find ourselves one moment closer to the day of Christ's appearing. Meanwhile, we must remain vigilant, for people will continue to look to *false Christs and false prophets* for inspiration and guidance as Jesus warned. In our day we all hear about apostate ministers who have renounced their ordination vows and presently reject Christ's teachings and God's Holy Word for what they claim is a better way, a newer way, or even multiple ways of reaching God. They blasphemously and willing distort God's Word. They purposely or perhaps ignorantly read it out of context. They ignore passages of which they do not approve. They search in vain for passages that validate their ridiculous interpretations as predicted in 1 Timothy 4:2, which states, they speak "lies in hypocrisy." In addition to pseudo-clergymen peddling a false gospel, we are also inundated with New Age charlatans who spread demonically inspired ideas about channeling, chanting, and other neopagan myths (1 Timothy 4:1). Because of this situation, Jesus warned that "the love of many shall wax cold" (Matthew 24:12).

> The same technology that makes global government a realistic threat makes it easier than ever to blanket the globe with God's truth.

But the news, even in these trying times, is not all bad. God is still in charge, and the following text informs us that the King of kings will soon arrive on the scene. Matthew 24:14 states, "And this gospel of the kingdom shall be preached in all the world for a witness unto all nations." Then and only then, Jesus said, shall the end—meaning the end of this age, not the world—come. At that moment, when the age of grace ends and the age of the

Millennium begins, our Lord and Savior appears with lightning speed in a blaze of glory (Matthew 24:27). Now the sign that precedes this event is presently in its initial stages. Do you realize that only in this age of modern communications and accelerated world travel can even the most isolated tribes globally be reached with the Word of God? It's happening! The same technology that makes global government a realistic threat makes it easier than ever to blanket the globe with God's truth. That's what our ministry—and this book about the Millennium—is all about: fulfilling the Great Commission. Did you know that more than 6,000 languages are spoken in our world today? Never before has the Bible been translated into so many of these tongues—even some spoken by obscure tribal groups. Certainly we are the generation about which Jesus spoke in Matthew 24:34. In this context, no signs have been more important than the rebirth of the state of Israel in 1948 (God's fig tree, Matthew 24:32; Joel 1:7; Hosea 9:10) and the recapturing of Jerusalem by the Jews in 1967. The very existence of Israel and Jerusalem's capture by these Israelites is a testament to the truth of the prophets and the fact that God keeps His word.

> "And they shall fall by the edge of the sword, and shall be led away captive into all nations: and Jerusalem shall be trodden down of the Gentiles, until the times of the Gentiles be fulfilled. And there shall be signs in the sun, and in the moon, and in the stars; and upon

the earth distress of nations, with perplexity; the sea and the waves roaring; Men's hearts failing them for fear, and for looking after those things which are coming on the earth: for the powers of heaven shall be shaken. And then shall they see the Son of man coming in a cloud with power and great glory. And when these things begin to come to pass, then look up, and lift up your heads; for your redemption draweth nigh." And he spake to them a parable; "Behold the fig tree, and all the trees; When they now shoot forth, ye see and know of your own selves that summer is now nigh at hand. So likewise ye, when ye see these things come to pass, know ye that the kingdom of God is nigh at hand. Verily I say unto you, This generation shall not pass away, till all be fulfilled." (Luke 21:24-32)

So the good news is that Jesus is returning, and this time, He will remain on earth to rule personally for one thousand years—*ten incredible, unrivaled centuries that will be as no other in the history of mankind*. However, there is even more excitement as we contemplate the fact that following the one thousand years, Christ is recommissioned to continue His earthly kingdom forever—in a world without end (Isaiah 45:17; Ephesians 3:21). Isaiah 9:7 declares, "Of the increase of his government and peace there shall be no end." Luke 1:33 adds, "And he shall reign over the house of Jacob for ever; and of his kingdom there shall be no end." That's why Yahweh the

Father says to Christ His Son, "Thy throne, O God, is for ever and ever" (Hebrews 1:8). Now if these texts are correct, and there is no doubt about it for they are God's Word, then this planet must continue to exist eternally. Is this found in Holy Writ? Definitely! Ecclesiastes 1:4 states, " . . . the earth abideth for ever." And Psalm 104:5 adds, "[God] laid the foundations of the earth, that it should not be removed for ever." Now since there are no contradictions in the Bible, and since we know that the six texts mentioning the end of the world are mistranslations of the Greek word *aion* meaning "age" not "world" (see appendix), it is easy to understand how Christ rules over the earth for one thousand years (Revelation 20:4), but then after the Millennium—when He is recommissioned—rules eternally (Revelation 11:15), and why believers rule and reign with Him for one thousand years (Revelation 20:4), but after the Millennium continue to reign with Him forever (Revelation 22:5). Now, and perhaps for the first time, do we understand why "the righteous shall inherit the land, and dwell therein for ever" (Psalm 37:29). Hallelujah! Heaven has finally been situated on earth forever and ever. Maranatha! "Even so, come, Lord Jesus" (Revelation 22:20).

APPENDIX

There are six texts in the New Testament that use the terminology "end of the world." They are Matthew 13:39, 40, 49; 24:3; 28:20; and Hebrews 9:26. In each of these instances a mistranslation of the Greek word *aion* occurred. *Aion* should be translated "age" rather than "world." For instance, when the disciples came to Jesus in Matthew 24:3, what they really asked was, "Lord, what shall be the sign of Thy coming, and of the end of the *age* of grace preceding Your earthly establishment of the Millennial Kingdom?"

The Bible never contradicts itself. Thus, the Greek word *aion,* meaning "age," is mandatory as the correct translation. Otherwise, the texts about to be studied, which deal with a world without end, would become meaningless. Since the Word of God is reliable and trustworthy, consider the following thought. In Matthew 24:3

the expression "end of the world" cannot be correct. Why? By turning the page, one finds Christ's coming to earth described (Matthew 25:31). When He appears to judge millions, He invites the redeemed to enter His glorious kingdom (verse 34). If the world were to end as translated in Matthew 24:3, there could be no earthly kingdom for one thousand years. I trust the following study will be spiritually beneficial.

"WORLD WITHOUT END"

Psalm 104:5	"Who laid the foundations of the earth, that it should not be removed forever"
Ecclesiastes 1:4	"The earth abideth forever"
Isaiah 45:17	"Ye shall not be ashamed nor confounded world without end"
Ephesians 3:21	"Unto him be glory in the church by Christ Jesus throughout all ages, world without end. Amen"

God's covenants, ordinances, and statutes are acted out eternally upon earth. Keep that in mind while studying the multiple texts below.

"EVERLASTING"

Genesis 9:16	"Everlasting covenant"

Genesis 17:7	"Everlasting covenant"
Genesis 17:8	"I will give unto thee, and to thy seed after thee, the land . . . for an everlasting possession"
Genesis 17:13	"Everlasting covenant"
Genesis 17:19	"Everlasting covenant"
Genesis 48:4	"I will give this land . . . for an everlasting possession."
Genesis 49:26	"Everlasting hills" (Impossible if the world should end.)
Leviticus 16:34	"Everlasting statute"
Leviticus 24:8	"Everlasting covenant"
2 Samuel 23:5	"Everlasting covenant"
1 Chronicles 16:17	"Everlasting covenant"
Psalm 41:13	"Blessed be the LORD God of Israel from everlasting, and to everlasting" (Both God and Israel are everlasting.)
Psalm 105:10	"Everlasting covenant"
Psalm 106:48	"Blessed be the LORD God of Israel from everlasting to everlasting"
Psalm 145:13	"Thy kingdom is an everlasting kingdom"

Isaiah 55:3	"Everlasting covenant"
Isaiah 56:5	"I will give them an everlasting name"
Isaiah 61:7	"Everlasting joy" (upon earth)
Isaiah 61:8	"Everlasting covenant"
Jeremiah 10:10	"He is the everlasting king" (on earth)
Jeremiah 32:40	"Everlasting covenant"
Ezekiel 16:60	"Everlasting covenant"
Ezekiel 37:26	"Everlasting covenant"
Daniel 4:3	"His kingdom is an everlasting kingdom"
Daniel 4:34	"[His] dominion is an everlasting dominion" (on earth)
Daniel 7:14	"His dominion is an everlasting dominion"
Daniel 7:27	"[His] kingdom is an everlasting kingdom"
Daniel 9:24	"To bring in everlasting righteousness" (on earth)
Luke 18:30	"In the world to come life everlasting" (This world is on earth.)

2 Peter 1:11	"The everlasting kingdom of our Lord and Saviour Jesus Christ" (on earth)

"ETERNAL"

Isaiah 60:15	"I will make thee an eternal excellency, a joy of many generation"
1 Timothy 1:17	"The King eternal" (This is when He comes as King of kings [Revelation 19:16].)

"FOR EVER"

Genesis 13:15	"For all the land which thou seest, to thee will I give it, and to thy seed for ever"
Exodus 12:14	"An ordinance for ever"
Exodus 12:17	"An ordinance for ever"
Exodus 15:18	"The LORD shall reign for ever and ever." (on earth)
Exodus 28:43	"A statute for ever"
Exodus 30:21	"A statute for ever"
Exodus 31:17	"It is a sign between me and the children of Israel for ever" (upon earth)

Exodus 32:13   "All this land that I have spoken of will I give unto your seed, and they shall inherit it for ever"

The majority of the following texts in the books of Leviticus and Numbers, dealing with temple sacrifices, will be fulfilled during the Millennium and then perpetually in the eternal kingdom upon earth.

Leviticus 6:18   "A statute for ever in your generations"

Leviticus 6:22   "A statute for ever"

Leviticus 7:34   "A statute for ever"

Leviticus 10:9   "A statute for ever throughout your generations"

Leviticus 10:15   "A statute for ever"

Leviticus 16:29   "A statute for ever"

Leviticus 16:31   "A statute for ever"

Leviticus 17:7   "A statute for ever"

Leviticus 23:14   "A statute for ever throughout your generations"

Leviticus 23:21   "A statute for ever in all your dwellings" (naturally on earth)

Leviticus 23:41   "A statute for ever in your generations"

Leviticus 24:3	"A statute for ever in your generations"
Numbers 10:8	"An ordinance for ever throughout your generations"
Numbers 15:15	"An ordinance for ever in your generations"
Numbers 18:8	"An ordinance for ever"
Numbers 18:11	"A statute for ever"
Numbers 18:19	"A statute for ever"
Numbers 18:23	"A statute for ever throughout your generations"
Deuteronomy 4:40	"The earth, which the LORD thy God giveth thee, for ever"
Deuteronomy 18:5	"Thy tribes . . . to minister . . . for ever" (naturally on earth)
Deuteronomy 28:46	"Thy seed for ever" (naturally on earth)
Joshua 4:7	"These stones shall be for a memorial unto the children of Israel for ever" (naturally on earth)
Joshua 14:9	Moses said, "The land whereon thy feet have trodden shall be thine inheritance, and thy children's for ever"

1 Samuel 13:13	"Would the LORD have established thy kingdom upon Israel for ever"
2 Samuel 7:16	"Thy throne shall be established for ever"
2 Samuel 7:24	"Thou hast confirmed to thyself thy people Israel [that they be] a people unto thee for ever"
2 Samuel 7:26	"Let the house of thy servant David be established" (For how long? See verse 29.)
2 Samuel 7:29	"Bless the house of thy servant, that it may continue for ever before thee . . . let the house of thy servant be blessed for ever"
1 Kings 2:45	"The throne of David shall be established . . . for ever" (That's on earth, Luke 1:32-33.)
1 Kings 9:5	"I will establish the throne of thy kingdom upon Israel [on earth] for ever"
1 Chronicles 16:36	"Blessed be the LORD God of Israel for ever and ever"
1 Chronicles 22:10	"I will establish the throne of his kingdom over Israel for ever"

1 Chronicles 23:25	"David said, The Lord God of Israel hath given rest unto his people, that they may dwell in Jerusalem for ever"
1 Chronicles 28:4	"King over Israel for ever"
1 Chronicles 28:7	"I will establish his kingdom for ever"
2 Chronicles 7:14, 16	"[I] will heal their land . . . that my name may be there for ever"
2 Chronicles 21:7	"The Lord would not destroy the house of David, because of the covenant that he had made with David . . . and to his sons for ever"
Psalm 10:16	"The Lord is King for ever and ever"
Psalm 29:10	"The Lord sitteth King for ever"
Psalm 45:6	"Thy throne, O God, is for ever and ever" (on earth)
Psalm 89:3-4	"I have sworn unto David my servant, Thy seed will I establish for ever" (naturally on earth)
Psalm 89:29	"His seed also will I make to endure for ever"

Psalm 89:35-36	"I will not lie unto David. His seed shall endure for ever"
Psalm 89:37	David's throne "shall be established for ever"
Psalm 146:10	"The LORD shall reign for ever, even thy God, O Zion"
Isaiah 9:7	"Of the increase of his government and peace there shall be no end." The throne of David is forever.
Isaiah 34:17	"They shall possess it for ever"
Isaiah 59:20-21	"The Redeemer shall come to Zion . . . from henceforth and for ever"
Isaiah 60:21	"They shall inherit the land for ever"
Jeremiah 7:7	"The land that I gave to your fathers, for ever and ever"
Jeremiah 17:25	"This city [Jerusalem] shall remain for ever"
Jeremiah 25:5	"The land that the LORD hath given unto you and to your fathers for ever and ever"
Ezekiel 37:25	"David shall be their prince for ever"

Ezekiel 43:9	"I will dwell in the midst of them for ever"
Daniel 2:44	His kingdom "shall stand for ever"
Daniel 7:18	"The saints of the most High shall take the kingdom, and possess the kingdom for ever, even for ever and ever"
Hosea 2:19	"I will betroth thee [Israel] unto me for ever"
Micah 4:5	"We will walk in the name of the LORD our God for ever and ever"
Micah 4:7	"The LORD shall reign over them in mount Zion from henceforth, even for ever"
Luke 1:33	"He shall reign over the house of Jacob for ever; and of his kingdom there shall be no end"
Hebrews 1:8	"Thy throne, O God, is for ever and ever" (on earth)
1 Peter 4:11	"Christ, to whom be praise and dominion for ever and ever" (on earth)

Revelation 1:6	"To him be glory and dominion for ever and ever" (on earth)
Revelation 11:15	"He shall reign for ever and ever" (on earth)
Revelation 22:5	"They shall reign for ever and ever" (on earth)

"FOR EVERMORE"

1 Chronicles 17:14	"I will settle him . . . in my kingdom for ever: and his throne shall be established for evermore" (on earth)
Psalm 106:31	"[His] righteousness unto all generations for evermore"
Psalm 121:8	"The LORD shall preserve thy going out and thy coming in from this time forth, and even for evermore"
Psalm 132:12	"Thy throne [is] for evermore"
Ezekiel 37:26	"It shall be an everlasting covenant. . . . I . . . will set my sanctuary in the midst of them for evermore"
Ezekiel 37:28	"My sanctuary shall be in the midst of them for evermore"

NOTES

Chapter 1

1. Joseph De Courcey, *Intelligence Digest,* 6 November 1999, The Stoneyhill Centre, Brimpsfield, Gloucester, UK.
2. J. Dwight Pentecost, *Things to Come,* (Grand Rapids, Mich.: Zondervan Publishing House, 1958), 376.
3. Ibid.
4. Dr. Nathaniel West, *The 1000 Year Reign of Christ,* (Grand Rapids, Mich.: Kregel Publishers, 1993), 414, 421.

Chapter 3

1. John F. Walvoord, *The Millennial Kingdom* (Grand Rapids, Mich.; Zondervan Publishing House, 1959), 15.

Chapter 6

1. Pentecost, *Things to Come,* 426–427.

Chapter 7
1. Pentecost, *Things to Come*, 494.

Chapter 9
1. Walvoord, *The Millennial Kingdom*, 324.
2. Pentecost, *Things to Come*, 577.
3. Ibid.

Chapter 10
1. John F. Walvoord, *Major Bible Prophecies*, (Grand Rapids, Mich.: Jack Van Impe Ministries, International, 1991), 406.

ADDITIONAL BOOKS FROM JACK VAN IMPE

Final Mysteries Unsealed

As he examines the prophecies of the book of Daniel, world-renowned teacher Jack Van Impe blows away the cobwebs of confusion and takes readers on a fascinating journey through past, present, and still-future prophecies.

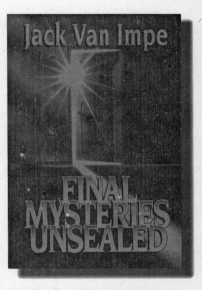

The Great Escape

With the decline of morality, a tumultuous political climate and occurrences of terrorism across the globe, Christians need to be reminded of the hope promised by God's Word. *The Great Escape* discusses specific details of the Great Tribulation and the Rapture.

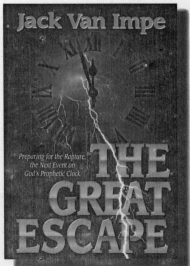

Revelation Revealed

Centuries before anyone could make sense of these fantastic warnings, the prophets declared that the mysteries of Revelation would not be understood until the Last Days. Verse by verse and chapter by chapter, Jack Van Impe reviews John's portrait of history's final climax.

2001: On the Edge of Eternity

In this eye-opening book, renowned evangelist and Bible teacher Jack Van Impe spells out the details of end-time prophecy, showing with pinpoint clarity how the "signs of the times" and the "end of the age" spoken by Jesus are being revealed before our eyes.